M000158712

RADIUS

REACHING ACROSS DIFFERENT INDUSTRIES UNCOVERING SOLUTIONS

The Universal Language of Business

By the best-selling author of *Third Circle Theory*,
Pejman Ghadimi

RADIUS
Reaching Across Different Industries Uncovering Solutions

Secret Entourage
www.SecretEntourage.com

Copyright © 2017 by Secret Entourage, LLC.
Secret Consulting, LLC
Chantilly, Virginia.

Createspace Paperback. ISBN: 978-0-9977610-2-3

Printed in United States of America.

Table of Contents

For my Uncle Parviz

Thank you for never forgetting about us.

Foreword by Fabio Viviani,
Serial Entrepreneur, Restaurateur and Celebrity Chef.

When I met Pejman a few years ago, I had no idea that I would to share this self-growth, awareness and fellowship journey with someone that was so much like me. You see, I'm different. Not better or worse than anyone; just different. Growing up I did not have anything: money, bragging rights, opportunities to a better life; all due to the circumstances my family and I were in. Every month that went by money was extremely scarce.

During my journey of becoming who I am today, I learned very early that many people's situations are harder than you could have ever imagined. I've encountered many individuals that are clueless about bad circumstances and focus on what they wish they had. Then get upset about it instead of being thankful for what they have that others don't and use that as a motivational springboard to propel themselves into their next move to a better life. So from a very young age I knew that being aware was extremely important and that who you are not defined by circumstances, but rather how you react and adapt to your circumstances will shape your future.

I've always believed that if you truly want to offer your expertise and services to others - with the only motive of being helpful, then many doors will open. Because I was taught to always expand my circle, make connections and rapport with others, I came across Secret Entourage. I reached out to someone from Secret Entourage via Instagram to offer one of my Chicago restaurants as location to host one of the Secret Entourage Academy Meet-Ups simply because I enjoyed the content provided on both, his business and personal, Instagram accounts. I offered my services free of charge just for the sake of meeting Pejman and stealing a few minutes of his time. I would have never imagined that we would've end up now talking almost every day; all due to sharing a vision for a better world and a passion to be better and do better.

I believe that anytime you find someone that is actually willing to spend his time in creating content and provide services to enhance people's life in any aspect or form is worth connecting with. I remember when I searched Pejman on Google; I discovered that besides all of the motivational and entrepreneurial videos he had done, he had also written several books. One of them in particular caught my attention: *The Third Circle Theory - Purpose through Observation*. I was immediately intrigued. Let's just say that after reading it three times in two short weeks, I came to the realization that Pejman was different; not better or worse than anyone I've met. Just different.

Growing up he did not have anything: money, bragging rights, opportunities to a better life; all due to the circumstances his family and he were in the middle of a war. His story was very similar than mine, but a lot harder actually. They escaped a revolution, moved from country to country, his mother worked very hard and finally they arrived to the United States. So for the first time I truly understood that circumstances never define who you are but rather give you an assessment of what your current situation is so you can act upon and improve it. In the *Third Circle Theory*, he provides an outline to understand that concept - how you can truly grow within and end up making the difference for others.

Once you become the best version of yourself, you will want to do great things. However, you will make mistakes, sweat blood and tears, and you will fall. I'm not trying to be negative, but as a person who currently operates six companies in five different industries with over 1,600 employees; built several million dollar businesses; and managed to get over one hundred million dollars in sales, I have collected more failures than successes. A resource is the mere vehicle to get there faster, but the lack of resourcefulness is the real reason why people don't succeed. Another factor to succeed is the ability to see beyond the circumstances you are in and figure out a plan, even if it is a not efficient one, where you can start and embrace the journey with the changes that come with it.

Imagine having a map that directs you to a successful journey and points out factors needed to get to your successful destination regardless of the industry you are? As the sequel, *R.A.D.I.U.S* will just lay it all out for you. I wish I would have read the *Third Circle Theory* sooner as it would have saved me ten years of struggle by helping realize that I'm the only person responsible for my own outcome. Same with *R.A.D.I.U.S*; if I would have read it twenty years ago, it would've saved me countless failures, headaches and defeats, which although necessary at time, they were also painful and very costly. *R.A.D.I.U.S* will teach you every single aspect that goes into creating a lasting legacy and an empire because regardless what you want to do with your life and in which sector you want to excel, the variables are always the same: yourself, people, product, market and anything else in between. Anyone serious about incrementing dramatically the chances of succeeding in life and creating a business that might turn into an empire needs to pick up a copy of this book.

Pejman is my long lost brother. Although we came from two different countries with different upbringings and zero idea about each other's existence, we now have a bond composed of mutual understanding and a high level of awareness - a type of awareness I've never seen before in any person I have ever met. While we value and enjoy what we materially have, such as the cars, houses, watches, etc., that doesn't define us. We like to be there for everybody by sharing our knowledge, enjoy being in the spotlight, and harvest the glory that came with our success; but our mission is a lot bigger. We are immensely small and insignificant compared to the purpose that we are trying to fulfill. Since I've read everything he was written and watched most of his videos, I can safely say that I am a better human being: a more focus business man as well as a better person overall. Sometimes you need to stop hating on the players and you just need to learn the game. *R.A.D.I.U.S.* will lay down the rules for you.

It's going to be a great journey, enjoy it.

Fabio Viviani

Preface:

When I wrote *Third Circle Theory*, my goal was never to teach people the best ways to go about starting a business or share how businesses succeed. Even though the content of *Third Circle Theory* evokes something within its reader that could lead to starting a business or taking on entrepreneurship, the main goal was to create a shift in the way people think. The way our thought process works can break boundaries that take us outside of our existing comfort zone, which is a necessity in order to break free from our previous limitations. We must first redefine our limitations, pushing ourselves farther away from that comfort zone before we can eventually live in a limitless world. It is important to understand that pushing our limitations starts in our minds, and it is no different than finding our purpose. That purposeful feeling in itself can be the necessary catalyst to make the break from those limitations set on us by our upbringing or the institution (society) we live in.

In the end, everything we know, believe, and feel is a fabrication of our mind, based upon a limitation set forth by our past experiences and environments. For example, the feeling of love or pain can also be translated in the same manner as our previous points of reference, helping us decipher what love or pain feels like and *giving context to any upcoming feelings and our reactions to it.* Our belief system, as explained in *Third Circle Theory,* is also an extension of our past experiences and can be easily tweaked and pushed by considering the context in of what we believe in. If everything is a fabrication based on our past environments and experiences, then we can definitely mold ourselves to the new environments in which we wish to belong and eventually, with enough consistency and hard work, achieve any goal and find our fit.

This ideology is the exact reason I wrote *RADIUS: How Visionaries Engineer Empires*.

The goal of this book is to help you understand the mechanics that connect business mastery to vision, understand the applicable theories that enable business masters to solve problems of massive magnitude over and over again, and, in many cases, continuously changing, disrupting, or improving industries. Understanding how the process works and the different components that come together in order to allow one person to disrupt an industry from both a business and an entrepreneurial angle.

Third Circle Theory's main focus is to help you understand your belief system and how to reach a level of fulfillment that allows you to unlock your purpose. It was, after all, the baseline for how visionaries are made. On the other hand, the goal of *RADIUS* is to help you understand how to translate your vision, belief, and talents into a business, brand and eventually an empire that establishes your legacy. In other words, if *Third Circle Theory* were considered the heart and soul of entrepreneurship, then *RADIUS* would be the skeleton of entrepreneurship.

I hope that you find as much value in *RADIUS* as you have discovered in *Third Circle Theory;* and remember that being an entrepreneur—or even attempting to become one—is an amazing act. One that not only redefines who we are or what we are capable of, but also shows us how powerful we can be as individuals and to others if we learn to work in a world without limitations or barriers, but rather with purpose.

- Pejman Ghadimi

Introduction to RADIUS - Definition

The dictionary definition:
Ra•di•us
/ ˈrādēəs/

noun

1. a straight line from the center to the circumference of a circle or sphere

2. a radial line from the focus to any point of a curve

3. ANATOMY

   the thicker and shorter of the two bones in the human forearm.

The above dictionary definition is accurate; nonetheless, truth is based solely on perception and therefore here is *my* definition:

noun

1. A straight line from your idea to the depth of how far you can take a business.

2. A radial line from the core focus of your belief to the outer perimeter of your reach.

3. The length of the lifeline of a business, as it pertains to its environment.

Though *"RADIUS"* may have many definitions, you will soon learn why it only stands for one thing: Reaching Across Different Industries Uncovering Solutions. By the end of this book, you will learn why the word also only represents one valid definition in business.

Understand that no matter what your focus in business is, what industry you work in, or what goals of world domination are churning in your head, your outcome boils down to how far you are willing to go to make it a reality. Therefore, my goal with *RADIUS* is to give you a step-by-step guideline to creating and executing a successful business, from idea to mass acceptance. *RADIUS* will focus on the evolution of business and its link to the visionary that creates it. Entrepreneurship is about innovation, about going where others haven't gone and creating order from chaos, which is why no matter how effective one is in their pursuit of becoming an entrepreneur, the same principles will never apply to the next person, even if they share similar circumstances. Being an entrepreneur requires someone to possess the ability to create their own path. They don't ask others for directions or a pathway to getting there. An entrepreneur is not a follower of the path others have taken.

Business on the other hand is quite different. There are certain elements that unite all businesses as universal. The outcome of a business can be traced back to the reason it succeeds or fails over the term of its life. Before we dive deep into the core fundamentals of business success, let us focus on the most important element in a business: *you*.

Understanding Human Learning Patterns

From an early age, society has taught us to seek a reward for just about anything we do. It is so apparent in our day-to-day behavior that we have even implemented this reward system with our pets. If they follow instructions and react to commands, they get a treat—the same way we have also been conditioned. From a very young age, we are wired with the same techniques: if we behave, we gain access to our very own toys. As we get older, the behavior continues in our education system. We take classes and learn subjects hoping to be rewarded with a diploma, which we believe will translate to landing a job and perhaps eventually becoming an expert in our field of educational focus.

The reward system does not end there. It continues infinitely as the major reward is money, which is a necessity in almost every aspect of what we do. Of course, there is nothing wrong with earning or seeking a reward for doing something right; however, the conditioning part that has been repetitively reinforced is preventing us from learning and expanding ourselves. This is partly because we expect something in exchange for all we do, including something as simple as learning. The learning process and knowledge itself is no longer viewed as its own reward. Self-education— based purely on inquisitiveness and a desire to grow instead of necessity—is rarely pursued. Yet, it is the greatest reward of all—as knowledge expands awareness.

By applying this logic to *RADIUS*, you realize that the reason you are most likely reading this book is not for its content or to raise your awareness, but rather because of your belief in the application to create self-benefit. Therefore, the return on your investment in reading this book will be based on the reward received rather than the content itself. Here is another example: If you read tons of information on the stock market, the reward you receive from the application of the learning is what makes you determine the importance of the information. In other words, if you make money immediately by trading stocks, then you consider the program a huge success; but if you get just information that teaches you without leading to any monetary results immediately following that learning, then you dismiss the program.

There is nothing wrong with applying yourself, learning, and eventually earning a reward, but you are limiting yourself with the ideology that the reward is the primary reason you seek and consume information. Everything we do when we identify opportunities comes from our own understanding and acceptance of the principles we are surrounded with every day. Therefore, by learning things that have no immediate compensation, we are expanding our reach and awareness even if not used immediately. We must not link our acceptance of the information to the amount of reward we accumulated from it. Our reality expands based on our learning. The real reward is to combine such learning with past and future experiences and create what we deem to be more choices and more possibilities. A reality that otherwise would not exist without such information being available to us in a previous setting. Understand that you consume information to enhance your awareness and give yourself broader perspective. As a result of this enhancement, you are able to identify opportunities much faster.

The best way to learn is to separate the idea from the reward. A simple example would be a web designer who may not have any interest in engineering or any of the processes associated with engineering, but exposes himself/herself to a book, which teaches the core of how engineering is done. There may be no need for him/her to do so as becoming an engineer is not of immediate interest at the moment, but in reality, the information consumed can and will be used in two manners in the future.

1. Providing context and the ability to understand as well as be understood. In a setting where other engineers may have need for a designer, someone with a contextual understanding of an industry is more educated and capable of holding a powerful conversation or helping others make relevant decisions.

2. Enabling the designer to understand the problems that face the engineering industry and may now allow the

person to solve a problem that requires design, but more importantly, allows the designer to understand the problems and requirements to creating solutions due to his/her intricate understanding of such industry.

Information holds value, even if no immediate association is made for the learner, because it enables your mind to remain open to new information. This is usually why babies who are exposed to many learning activities in their first five years tend to do better academically than others who are only offered games in their earlier years.

Understanding the Importance of Purpose

Being purposeful enables a person to push the boundaries of possibilities both internally and externally. It is within those precious moments where we believe that we are fulfilling our purpose, that we understand how to survive the bad times in business, or even take chances that might often seem ridiculous to those who are watching from the outside.

Purpose is an internal feeling that drives us forward, makes us work harder and empowers us to reach new heights in business and in life. A business itself has a purpose, one that plays a much more significant role in the greatest scheme of things. Business is the vehicle to entrepreneurship to reach the masses and the best way for a visionary to bridge the gap between vision and application.

The Timeline of the Universe

In our current state of minds, we are taught to consider the idea that each and every one of us has a timeline: a beginning, a middle, and an end, just like everything else in life. That timeline focuses on the belief that we each equally matter as human beings.

The universe itself has its own timeline, and all of us play a significant role within it. The difference is we play a much smaller role in the bigger picture than we think; nevertheless it is an important one. The thought behind business purpose is that business is not only the creation of a person to find purpose, but the ability to impact and serve millions of people. This action changes our personal sense of purpose as we evolve while giving others the ability or opportunity to discover their purpose as well. The opportunity to innovate is very much real and the baseline from which many of today's empires are formed. Depending on how far we carry out our reach, we ultimately impact more people and create more opportunities for the universe's timeline to continue moving forward.

From Business to Entrepreneurship, and Back

I always discuss the importance of mastering business before taking on entrepreneurship, as there is tremendous value in understanding the mechanics of how money flows, and how everything works together (customers, leaders, companies, products, and marketing) in order to create a successful business. Business and entrepreneurship are distinctly different, despite being divided by a very thin line: business is about profit, while entrepreneurship is about the creation of value. Every business at some point or another must become entrepreneurial in nature in order to grow past the point of trading time for money. The business owner must be the catalyst for such transformation, envisioning the change that needs to happen and driving the action to make it happen.

On the other hand, every entrepreneurial venture eventually must become a business, growing past the start-up and becoming accepted as a viable company. Just like trying to figure out whether the chicken came before the egg, which one comes first in this scenario—business or entrepreneurship?

From the entrepreneurship phase, an idea's or concept's core can provide tremendous value to the world it serves. Yet, it eventually will reach a level where the idea must be commercialized in order to become part of society, rather than being introduced as an alternative to an existing solution. Facebook and Myspace, for example, started as specific social networks geared to college students and music, respectively. Despite having made a name for themselves and creating tremendous value to such groups, these sites needed to be engineered to appeal to the general public in order to be embraced as the new way to interact with each other online. If these websites had not been changed to adapt to these markets, they concepts would have remained limited to those segments.

In order for those ventures to enter our culture and become part of it, both of them had to create revenue continuously because money is the measure of success for society. It is also the number one reason why people do or don't do something. Letting go of the innovation plus focusing on the idea of innovating the business side is the necessary transition every entrepreneur must make in order to grow what once started: a small venture into a brand that can become eternal in nature. For instance, Elon Musk's Tesla started as an entrepreneurial venture of saving the environment, which was then converted into a business model to support its mission and allow mass public adoption. The survival and growth of Apple, as today's most powerful company, came from its ability to innovate an industry dominated by what was perceived as non-user-friendly technology. Steve Jobs drove innovation in the company, with the revolutionary outcomes—iTunes, iPod, iPhone, iPad—creating a brand that is synonymous with innovation.

Every entrepreneur must accept that without their ventures becoming a successful business, it will not grow beyond its dependency on the founder.

From the business side, the primary goal remains to make money in a profitable, sustainable manner. Nonetheless, at some point, a business becomes stale from the simple mindset of "the more people you serve, the more money you make" and focusing on better serving people, rather than looking for additional customers. Quality, not quantity, should be the driving force.

The business owner at this stage can make a choice to remain in his comfort zone and try to make as much money as he can for as long as he/she can, or instead look ahead and be innovative in his thinking by investing time in building systems that enable him later to remove himself from the equation to still continue to grow the business into a brand. A restaurant follows this thinking when expanding into a franchise operation. In one restaurant, you can sell food to a limited group of patrons. McDonald's was able to not only create and perfect the franchising model, but also master the art of commercial real estate. Nowadays, most people open restaurants and fail, whereas McDonald's guarantees its franchisor's success because the company has understood more than just how to serve fast food to people. It has become entrepreneurial in nature and a household name worldwide by leveraging two different business models to guarantee its success and highly decrease its chances of failure.

Whichever way you start, understand this transition. It plays a part of both entrepreneurship and business, and will impact you no matter what industry you're in or how you account for your own personal success.

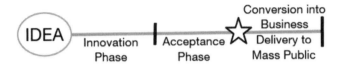

Five Pillars of Entrepreneurship and Business

Every business follows a cycle of specific elements, regardless of its success or failure. My goal is to help you understand *why* things occur as they do, so that you have a clearer vision of your own personal roadmap.

There are five core pillars in the evolution of business and entrepreneurship.

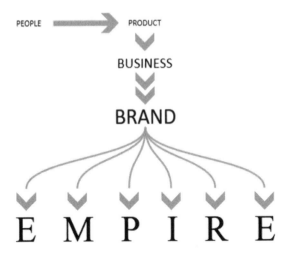

People

People are perhaps the most powerful and yet neglected pillar by most business owners and entrepreneurs. They fail to see that, without people, there cannot be any business or success. People—you, your team, and your customers—are the core foundation of any business. The majority of businesses fail in their first year because of the owner's lack of understanding of himself, his customers, the target market, and those around him. If you don't understand the wants, needs, and motivations of these people, you will not be able to effectively address them. Many business people may say they are not people-centric or understand people, but it is not your misunderstanding of people and their behaviors but rather your lack of understanding of yourself. Your level of self-awareness is a fundamental part of what we discussed in *Third Circle Theory*. If you lack self-awareness, you won't succeed much or fully understand this book.

There is no shortcut to understanding people. It is a skill that develops with time and experience. Costco is notorious for having mastered this power, both internally (the team) and externally (the customers). Everything this retailer does is about selling, and it stems from the psychology of people as shoppers and consumers—how they interact with each other and with the products. Costco understands the need for customers to save money, and knows exactly what products their customers want to spend money on. More importantly, they understand their employees enough to create environments that allow them to foster their talents and become better employees by connecting to customers better. Giving their employee's authority and the right environment to uphold such authorities gives them the capacity to connect customers to employees and employees to the brand. This people-centric approach has helped them grow and become the brand that is recognized worldwide.

Product

Regardless of what you sell, the product (or service) remains the core of why and how you survive and grow. Therefore, your product has to be something that is forever being improved and adapted to an ever-changing environment. The product isn't always perfect and may not even be good in its early stages. Products that solve real problems hold much more value to the masses, but sometimes they are very often the worst products out there in their early entry phases. Most people who venture to fix mass market problems have no roadmap or data to help them understand how people will interact with or accept their new product or any variations of it. The products created are often amazing in ideology and terrible in execution because of the lack of data from previous or existing competitors. The point of a product, however, is its success in actually solving a problem. Of course, you need to be flexible and responsive with a new product—to quickly perfect and continuously work on your—to build toward a massively accepted solution. Just remember that, while most products are intended to solve a problem, that particular issue may not be accepted by the public as a real problem. Long before the smartphone came along, there was the personal digital assistant (PDA). In 1993, Apple launched the Newton, and it was a massive failure, because people didn't see the need for this gadget. In 1997, the Palm Pilot changed their thinking by clearly demonstrating the value of a handheld electronic device. The market embraced the concept, which paved the way for the iPhone smartphone in 2007.

While smartphones existed for quite some time before the iPhone came along, the features with smartphones were only limited. The general public never knew that the real problem behind the evolution of cell phones was based on the carriers (e.g., Verizon, AT&T) and not the phone's capacity. The phones weren't evolving because carriers were preventing non-revenue-making features from being introduced and therefore limited the advancement of the phone's capacity. What Apple did was not create the perfect smartphone, but rather introduce a solution that, over the years, became a great smartphone. Never a perfect product, but the app marketplace allowed phones to connect to more possibilities, while preventing carriers from their greedy restriction of the product's growth.

Business

When the right people come together with the idea for a service or product, then a business is conceived. A business is created when a person understands both people and product, and as a result, establishes a way to connect the two. By linking them together, a business becomes profitable and thrives, but if people and product are not compatible, then the business fails. The connection between the two is often the catalyst for the growth or survival of a business. Whenever a business fails, we blame either people or product, but not very often analyze how the product and people interacted on all levels as the root of the failure. When people believe and understand the product, and the product actually solves a problem, the optimum connection occurs and it allows a business to rise to profitability. The continuation of a business's growth is connected to how well the product and people continue to evolve within the its dynamics, which adds a very powerful variable—known as money.

The effective collaboration of people and product is needed to grow an industry, but don't forget that appropriately factoring in money is necessary to allow the business to evolve into a ***brand***.

The finance industry does a marvelous job at creating a bridge that allows people to reach their product, which is money. The best part is that the product, in most cases, doesn't even belong to the bank; in other words, the bank is the *product* itself, and money is the *solution* that people want.

Brand

When a business has mastered the execution of its product and connected it to people in a seamless manner, it has reached a level of profitability above and beyond that of a simple business. The idea of *significant profit* prompts the entrepreneur to look backwards and connect the dots. Understanding the path to success enables a business owner to look forward with something powerful— *process*.

Process is simply understanding how people, product, and business intertwine. With this knowledge, you can duplicate a successful process with new products and new people, in new verticals or new commodities. Because the process that has made it successful and accepted by people is duplicated in all those verticals, the idea of trust appears, due to the consistency experienced by people when interacting with new commodities. This creates a feeling of comfort in people, and establishes the traits that make a brand trustworthy.

The three traits that can be found and seen across every item or vertical (store sales are a vertical are reliability, simplicity, and design. This trio is what makes Apple a super-brand and why millions line up to buy new Apple products, knowing that their expectations will be met without even understanding the new product or its functionality. At Secret Entourage, we have made photography, design, and lifestyle the three components you will see in everything we do. From success stories to social media, you can expect to be motivated, educated, and inspired through those three factors.

As we released Secret Academy (a new vertical you might say), we made sure that it stayed true to that formula as well.

Brands are created when process becomes **mastered** and is duplicated properly over various verticals. Brands become *accepted* by people when trust is created and that process become obvious, even on a subconscious level.

Empire

Last, but not least, comes the evolution of a brand into an empire. When a brand expands through so many verticals that it has earned trust, regardless of what it undertakes within that space, the brand gives way to potentially becoming an empire.

An empire is simply defined as an entity that dominates in every vertical within its space and, in some cases, outside of its space. Facebook is attempting to become an empire by acquiring every possible social network that it competes with, offering various types of social reach, but ultimately keeping it all under on brand. Apple is also doing the same by now becoming involved in the financial sector (Apple Pay), even though it had never before played in that space. For a brand to become an empire, the people running the business must be confident enough that their user base will follow them across any platform. They must feel assured that their understanding of process is so streamlined that it can work anywhere at any time, and in any space.

Beats Audio started as headsets but has expanded into the automotive space. With its acquisition by Apple, Beats has not only gained access to a broader tech industry, but also has allowed Hollywood and Silicon Valley to get closer; ultimately allowing Apple to once again branch out from its business realm. An empire is a powerful entity that comes with a significant level of influence and can give birth to innovation or kill ideas in seconds. It is the ultimate reach in business and it is nothing more than engineering a perfect system where

(People + Product + Process) x Verticals = RADIUS (Reaching Across Different Industries Uncovering Solutions)

SECTION 1: THE STORY

I don't consider myself an author, or even someone who understands any aspect of literary art, yet I find it my obligation to write in order to share a message. In my life, I had yet to read a book before I was able to make *Third Circle Theory* an Amazon best seller. I don't consider myself to be a great writer, or one that has a distinct style, despite having now written eleven books to date. I never finished college, and during my short-lived college year, I hardly paid attention to any classes. My book editor will frequently attempt to correct each page of every book I write, yet I often decline to change the wording within my book as I feel that the message would lose its value if someone changes its interpretation while making it grammatically perfect. I have shared my story many times in numerous articles, interviews and podcasts, but the story I will share with you in this book will not be one of success or failure; it will certainly be very different than the story you hear me tell during those interviews.

Throughout this book, you will learn about my business life, but primarily learn everything you need in order to successfully adapt to any business playing field, no matter what industry you are in. While I am telling you a rather long story, I will most importantly be teaching you about key components that made me who I am today and enabled me to understand business through a rather interesting lens—one that involves a high level of awareness, belief, and the ability to connect the dots forward through vision.

A Vague Memory...

I can't forget the memory I have of when I was three years old, sitting on top of my father's shoulders in a cold basement with hundreds of other people. I remember how quiet it was and how you could clearly hear everyone breathing. No one spoke a word. We had a small view of the street from a tiny window made of bars on the right side of the basement. We could see a chaotic mob running around with no direction or purpose. Then, five minutes or so later, a bright light came from above, very bright and with an extremely loud noise—so bright and loud that for about the next five minutes, I couldn't see or hear anything. That deafening moment was the quietest I have ever experienced.

Once the effects of the light and noise wore off, the screams started coming from the streets—loud cries of despair, hopelessness, and misery. Many of the buildings that had been there were crumbled to the ground. I couldn't make sense of what I was hearing or looking at. Years later, I asked my mother about that memory, and she answered, "the war in Iran."

It turned out that the war between Iran and Iraq had led to airstrikes forcing people to hide in basements to be as safe as possible. What I had witnessed was a missile demolishing the tall building next to ours. It was a good thing that I was too young to understand what has happening around me then. It stays with me as a memory rather than a scar.

The same year, we escaped the war and found ourselves in France as refugees. First, we settled in my uncle's basement, then in a studio with my single mother. I used to watch my mother go to work every day from six in the morning to ten at night. She would leave me food to warm-up in the microwave when I was alone and take me to work on days when there was no school. In France back then, school buses didn't exist, so I used to walk to school and home again daily. As a child, my biggest desire was to be picked up from school by my mother, just like all the other kids who were always greeted and picked up by parents when the school day was done. Years passed and many birthdays came and went. To this date, one of the most powerful memories I still have is one that happened during those years: my mother stealing toys for me at a local supermarket because she simply couldn't afford them as we barely had money for food. She would repeatedly get caught, warned, and let go. I understood why she did it but I didn't want the security man to come back out to get her, so I simply stopped asking for toys as time went on. Finally, we moved into a one-bedroom apartment that made things a bit better and eventually even got our own car, which was later stolen. What are the odds, right? From my bedroom window, I used to watch my neighbor wash his brand new Ford Fiesta. The car was black on black and had a vinyl graphic on the hood as if someone had spilled red paint on the front of it. It was the coolest thing I had seen and for some reason, I really liked that car. For years, it remained a fixation for me, or you could say an *inspiration*. That desire was the reason why, to this day, I enjoy washing my own cars.

My mother started her own business with the help of her brother. It was a digital imagining company that helped people do photocopies and sold films for cameras (as digital cameras were still far away). Their camera inventory was excellent. I used to hold and touch them, but couldn't own one. I spent the majority of my off-school days in the basement of that business, doing homework and watching my mother work. I always observed how much she cared for her clients and helped even the weirdest or rudest clients.

The highlight of her years was the day, every six months, when we went to the embassy in an effort to get a visa to come to the United States. This ritual began from the time we arrived in France and so every six months, we would go the embassy. We would take the subway and walk for two hours, only to be told that we would never be granted a visa to the United States. They suspected that she would never return to France if they granted her a visa. They were right. My mother's destination goal was the United States.

After nine years of trying, we were finally granted that visa, giving us only two weeks to buy a plane ticket and leave. Apparently, it was done as a way to make sure we wouldn't just leave to stay forever in United States, as no one in their right mind would leave behind their apartment, furniture, business, and a cat, especially knowing our financial situation was far from comfortable. They obviously underestimated my mother and her will power. We gave away my cat and most of our furniture away and left the business to my uncle.

As if I had a choice, I agreed to go under one condition: I would get a Sega Saturn as soon as we reached our destination (for younger generation readers, the Sega Saturn was an early version of a PlayStation). This was my only request, and yes, I sold out for a gaming console. To my credit, the console had legendary games for its time. This was the era they introduced 3D gaming to the world, which was quite an important era for the world of gaming. As my childish and irrelevant demands were met, we left France for another beginning in Los Angeles, California, to meet my mother's younger brother, Parviz, who had been separated from her for over 20 years. Because I hadn't seen my father since I was three years old, I never had a father figure until I met Parviz. He inspired me and would later be a pivotal reason I succeeded in life and business as he was an important executive in a luxury hotel in Glendale, California at that time. We settled in an apartment close to the hotel where he worked.

My mother was true to her word and bought me a Sega Saturn. I got to play it on a 60-inch TV, which I had never before seen in my life. I had my own room, a big screen TV, and the latest video games. We had access to my uncle's Ford Probe, which was a popular car during that time. As far as I was concerned, we had finally made it.

My mother opened up a coffee shop, called Metro Burger. It failed miserably after a year or so, but it did allow us to get social security numbers. And even though the cards said "not valid for work", having a social security number was better than nothing.

Just when my life had reached its greatest peak of fun, I was once again reminded that perhaps poverty was more fitting for now. My uncle Parviz lost his executive job and we had to move all the way to Fairfax, Virginia, to live with my other uncle, Ahmad, who owned a restaurant there. Once more, long gone were the days of no worries. The goal was that both my uncle Parviz and mother would work with my uncle Ahmad once we arrived in Virginia. We used a large U-Haul truck to travel from California to Virginia in eight days and the memories we made during that trip were unique, but priceless for sure.

Shortly after arriving, we found ourselves back in a basement, my mom got a job as a cashier at my uncle Ahmad's restaurant in Washington D.C., and my uncle Parviz started to work at a hotel two hours away from the house. Things did eventually get better as my uncle Parviz got promoted quickly. We finally got a small townhome, and I started to go to school. Life continued.

At the beginning of the school year, I didn't fit in. I wasn't popular, didn't speak very well, wasn't great at academics, and didn't take a liking to any extracurricular activities. I did excel in art, but did not have any interest in the subject. I always felt lost and, come to think of it, never understood why I was even going to high school. One thing I did do every day was walk through the parking lot and look at the cars, particularly a red Saleen Mustang parked in the faculty lot, which always made me wondered how a teacher could afford one of those "cool" cars. I was 14 years old and started growing distant of the idea of fitting in, so I almost felt that it was best if I didn't try at all. Since I didn't have any hobbies and didn't do very well in sports, I decided to instead help my mother by looking for a job. The work permit I had allowed me to work limited hours while I still was 14. I applied to all places that were within walking distance from my house, from the local McDonald's to the antique store, only to be told over and over that my social security number was not valid for work. I didn't have any work experience, but when I was 12 years old, I had worked for my mother in California at her coffee shop delivering pizzas using my bicycle. Yes, this is how rough times were—the coffee shop was selling pizzas on the side. I knew that my work ethic wasn't great, but since I had nothing better to do, I was willing to put in the effort. Because work wasn't available for a 14-year-old immigrant, it only made sense to focus on chores from the neighborhood, such as washing cars, cleaning houses, and mowing lawns. Cleaning houses was harder than it seemed and a short-lived venture for me. Mowing lawns was limited due to the small amounts of grass all the townhomes in the neighborhood had. By process of elimination, washing cars became the next best thing for me. It started with a $5 car wash, which might have seemed like slave work to many people, but it ended up becoming a 40-million-dollar business for me! I printed flyers and gained enough interest to make twenty-dollars a day, which better than nothing. Even though the business was slow due to cold weather and people working during the day, I still managed to make fifteen to twenty dollars a day after passing out flyers for a month.

A few weeks later, while walking through the high school cafeteria, I got my first taste at being recruited. Two interesting individuals in the customer service field were passing flyers and offering twelve dollars per hour. Both were pretty excited about talking to me, and the excitement was mutual. I noticed that I was the only one talking to them, which made me wonder if perhaps my classmates knew something I did not or maybe I was too naïve to realize I was being recruited. Regardless, I inquired more about the job and was told it would a phone-based position doing customer service. In the end, I would have killed for a job, and I agreed to work for a one-day paid trial.

One of the key lessons I learned then is not the power of naïvité, but rather the accuracy of Thomas Edison's saying, *"opportunity is missed by most people because it is dressed in overalls and looks like work"*. Their flyer clearly said twelve dollars per hour and the minimum wage back then was five dollars and fifty cents per hour. That meant they were paying almost three times more for high school students, yet no one had any interest as the job revolved around telemarketing. It was work to me, and the idea that it paid three times more than what I could have earned at McDonald's made it a no-brainer. The goal was not to be comfortable, have a job I loved at the age of 14, and start a career; the goal was to make an income, so aligning the goal with the offer made perfect sense to me.

When I went for my first day as an official employee, I decided to change my strategy and showed my work permit from my high school instead of my social security card. I stuck to my story that as a 14-year-old, I had no idea where my social security card was, but I had memorized my number. I relied on the fact that if my social security card was not physically seen, then no one could know if the number was valid for work or not. Also, because the company was relatively small, my chances of getting the job without providing a copy of it was high. I was asked for my social security card a few times after and I kept telling the same thing—I didn't know where it was. Ultimately, the administrative people stopped asking for it. This was my first and only opportunity to start working and making money, so I knew that losing this job meant being unemployed, and perhaps, for a long time.

The idea of losing my job before even starting made me realize the importance of my employment, and my need to excel in performance. I had no idea what to do, how to do it, and certainly didn't have the skills to manage it. I decided to take it one step at a time and eventually rid myself of this fear of failure before it even happened. I realized that most of the unjustified fear was in my head and there was be no reason to think I was at risk of losing my job. I decided to focus on the work. I was given a list of handwritten leads to call. I was told that the leads were collected by canvassers who went door-to-door so that the company could follow up. I obtained my first lead, whose name was Dick Black. Without thinking twice that it might be a joke, I called the guy and simply asked if Mr. Black Dick was home, and I got an immediate hang-up.

Not understanding what telemarketing was and how consumer behavior adapted to this profession, this time I called back asking if Mr. Dick was home. I was hanged up on once more. Then followed by an approximate eighty hang-ups within three hours. At the beginning, I wondered why others weren't working hard and only made an average of fifty calls a day, when I made that in an hour. However, after that first interaction, I understood that no one believed in the work, strategy, or the results. I swiftly comprehended that no one was taking their job seriously. Unlike them, my options were limited as this was the only job I could find, so it was necessary for me to focus on the work and not on what I liked. Every day I worked, I would continuously make over a hundred calls, even though I was hanged up on over a hundred times each week. After my first two weeks, my first check was for 260 dollars, which gave me this feeling of accomplishment and reaffirmation that being hanged up on all this time wasn't that bad at all. I began to care more for my job as it became more real when I held my first check in my hands.

I kept getting hang-ups countless times, to the point that I became comfortable with being rejected. Every time someone hung up on me was like a punch in the stomach, but each punch increased my tolerance for emotional pain and my downtime between each call decreased significantly. As result, I was able to continue making more calls and actually try to close sales. An important but simple lesson I learned here was that even when we don't have the exact answers as to what to do to be successful, it is better to be moving forward practicing what we do know rather than remaining stagnant in search of direction. Practice enables momentum, but stagnation can break that same motion. And so, I kept moving forward.

After weeks of calling the same leads I was given, I decided to stop following the same call script without thinking first, since I wasn't having any luck closing sales. I was always observant, which made me notice which sales employees closed the most leads. I spent a few days just asking questions of individuals who were running the appointments we were setting for them. I simply asked to understand what the product was, and more importantly what the process was. I also inquired about which leads of theirs closed the fastest versus those that took the longest. I wanted to understand if we sold more windows, more siding or more roofs; after a few days of shadowing and analyzing, I comprehended that understanding customer behavior and need would be the key to closing sales. I wanted to close a sale, so I didn't feel useless but also because it paid a commission of 10% of the sale, which on average was $9,000 per ticket and would increase my paycheck immensely. Closing one sale per week would mean I would quadruple my income.

This is when I learned that the key to making money was not to work several hours a week, but rather to maximize the impact of your work within those hours. I later used this strategy to move up six promotions in three years in a Fortune 500 bank. I understood a crucial lesson related to making money that has stayed with me for over 20 years when I saw how significant it was to close better sales. I learned the law of supply and demand.

The Law of Supply and Demand

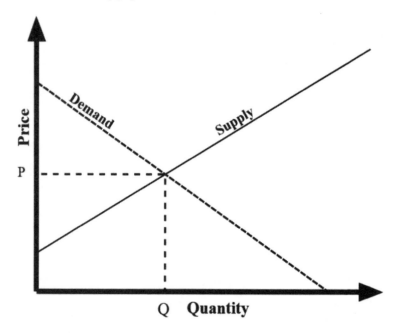

It is known that when supply is down and demand is up, price goes up. The same can be said of the opposite: too much supply and not enough demand, price goes down. This is the typical definition of *supply and demand* and its correlation with price. But supply and demand goes way beyond just impacting price. With high demand, there is an opportunity for anyone who can create a supply of what is needed and this was what I learned that day. Taking the same equation, one can simply replace the need for something on one side, with the accessibility on the other and it would create a similar effect in price and or willingness to buy. So, if there is a need and no access, there is a price increase; and if there is no need and yet there is access, a lower price plays a more significant role in closing the sale.

The goal then became to either find people with a need, or to show them that they have a need—even if they didn't know it yet. This changed my entire thinking about the way I was attempting to set appointments to sell people home remodeling. They had no need or reason to buy, unless the price was significantly lower than usual, creating an urgency in making a decision. Since we weren't really discounting prices, I had to come up with a way to find an opportunity to identify a possible need. First, I changed my pitch and focused on telling people on the phone that their neighbors were getting an estimate because their roofs were leaking. And since their home was in the same neighborhood, we could also look at it for free to see if it made sense for them to redo their roof, too. I received more positive engagement using this strategy; nonetheless, it hardly increased my sales ratio. That made me realize that I was missing something in my own formula. I was overlooking the fact that people might actually be in need of renovations, but they had no access to getting started. The concept was simple: What if there was a need, but the high price created a lack of access for the buyer? What if people who needed a new roof and were willing to pay for it, couldn't afford the cost? I realized that there is a significant opportunity everyone in the office was missing.

Customers who had experienced natural disaster damages, such as hail, strong wind, or heavy snow, had a need for a new roof and didn't even have to pay for it. With that insight, I had not only solved the need, but also the lack of monetary access by letting them know that their insurance would pay for the renovation. I investigated how insurance companies worked. It could take 90 days to get a claim paid and to find a company to fix the damage, especially when insurance companies were backed up for weeks (a common situation after a natural disaster). Waiting months to fix a necessity you didn't even need to pay for made no sense. This was my first taste of solving problems for people. Although I was far from being an entrepreneur, I figured that my best bet was to call people and to offer them an estimate before their insurance adjuster came out. Having that estimate in hand would expedite the process, and we could be paid directly.

Because I could see past the obstacles experienced by many of my co-workers and then focus on a solution, I was making over $2,500 a week in commissions as a telemarketer for months and growing the entire office in sales. In total, I made an average of $10,000 per month, which was a lot of money for a 15-year-old; but this is how I understood leverage at a very young age.

The Power of Leverage

Most people make money to buy possessions and, by doing so, they miss out on the reality that making money creates leverage, which is something I learned early on, the hard way.

When I was about 16 years old, my financial life was in a very good place, but my social life, not so much. I tended to be isolated and didn't have many friends. Back then, I used to wear khaki pants with tucked-in, Hawaiian shirts accessorized with a brick-size cell phone on my hip, so I guess that made me an easy target to be picked on by bullies. On the second day I was bullied, I realized the importance of leverage when I took in the fact that I was making $10,000 a month, which was clearly enough to offer someone a job. No one knew how much money I made, but I knew that someone else's time could be worth six dollars an hour, so using fifty dollars a week as a budget, I found the largest and strongest guy in school. I convinced him to make sure that next time someone picked on me, to make it an example of the consequences. The problem was solved with a mere $200 a month, which was less than two percent of my income.

Buying and playing video games was fun, but there were only so many games to buy, which left plenty of money in my savings account after each month. I had extra money that allowed me to hire my illegal immigrant friends, who could not work anywhere else for a fraction of their worth. It was not evil; it was business. I knew what others, who faced similar issues as I did, were willing to do to work, so I used the same system of supply and demand by leveraging two of my friends to start a side business.

Instead of buying more unnecessary things, I decided to save for a nice car while I was leveraging my ability to be in more than one place at once by starting this small side business of detailing and fixing up cars.

I returned to the place where it all started with me selling roofs and siding in Fairfax, Virginia. The office was part of a large building that housed about 600 offices and another 1,000 residences, all of which shared one enormous parking lot. I've always paid attention to my surroundings. While I was at work, I realized that there were many cars in the parking lot. I noticed that there was no hose and no place to wash your car anywhere near the building. The cars were surrounded by trees, which meant that many of them were covered with pollen and sap almost all the time. These thoughts gave birth to the idea that perhaps washing people's cars while they were working could be a convenient service that they would pay for, especially if it saved them an hour waiting at the local car wash.

I was, after all, already familiar with washing cars in my neighborhood a few years back. Now, I also had the resources: two unemployed immigrant acquaintances whom I could bring with me after school to help clean cars. So, by recycling the same resources, I put them both to work, with very little expense—cleaning supplies and towels.

I didn't want to be in the car wash business. I didn't know anything about cars, except that I washed a lot of them when I couldn't get a job a few months ago. I figured, why not make my friends come help and make a few bucks? While I couldn't do the work—since I already had a job—it made sense to leverage their time. As a result, I made some money getting a piece of the pie, rather than not making any money. The point was, like I had previously said, that if I were going to spend forty hours at work, I was going to spend it by making as much as I could.

I launched the business started by passing out flyers that advertised five- to ten- dollar car wash rates. After weeks of trying to drum up customers, the service came to life as the clients warmed up to the idea and utilized us weekly.

At the time, I was working an easy, part-time job making an average of $7,500 to $10,000 a month, and had my very first business making $500 a week, most of which I paid to my workers. Even if I were making an extra hundred dollars a week, I wasn't actually working for it, so it wouldn't matter.

After months of cleaning cars, people brought up further needs, such as light bulb changes, restoration of headlights, tire change, along other maintenance requests that would be convenient to get done while at work. I saw a great opportunity here, so I contacted my good friend, Scott, who was a mechanic at Honda, I asked him to join me and fix cars with me. The business grew from washing cars to becoming the go-to place for everything related to car maintenance in that complex, like an automotive handyman service.

People weren't necessarily paying for expertise; they were paying for convenience. From both the commercial and residential side, we were getting customers and everyone loved my two worker friends. No one at my work knew that I was the person behind the operation until months later. This gig continued for a few years while my success at my regular job also kept growing. I was getting promoted every four to five months. By the time I graduated high school, I was the director of that very same company where I had started working illegally. *That's crazy that he juggled school w/ this!*

Since my leverage was allowing me to buy video games just as much as it was allowing me to push my business forward, I set my sights on larger things, such as a nice townhome and nice cars. The opportunity to buy my very first car became a life-changing moment with a very important lesson attached to it. You know that money wasn't something that we had a lot of, but thankfully for me poverty also was no longer in the picture. My uncle owned a 1989 Ford Probe, a car that I liked very much, but it was difficult for me to be the fourth person sharing the car.

One of my unforgettable memories was the night my uncle Parviz asked me if I was ready to go car shopping. As a 16-year-old, I was thrilled to get my first car. We were not just going to test drive any car, but a 1997 Camaro Z28, which was one of my dream cars. That evening, the test drive was amazing and the excitement at an all-time high, but it soon ended when I was politely informed by my uncle that the car we were test driving was not for me, but for him. He continued by stating that when it was time to get a car for me, he would gladly help my mom purchase a Toyota Corolla—which was a good and reliable car for a teenager. Even though his intention to partly pay for the car was appreciated, my taste for cars had now evolved, due to the test drive and the incredible car that I was sitting in. He said something that did not only stick with me, but resonated as the fundamental principle that helped me become who I am today: "When you seek help, you get the basics. If you want the best. you have to earn it."

Obviously, I was not getting the car I wanted. By not doing so, I knew that I never wanted to hear someone else tell me what I could or could not have. This was more than enough for me to decide that hard work was going to be the only method of getting a nice car, and the push I needed to care for more than just my basic survival at my telemarketing job.

This car fiasco changed my view on life as it reinforced the necessity of constantly pushing the limitations I was given to the point where all these things I wanted would be within my reach.

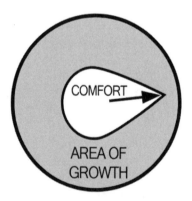

These tools are right in front of all of us. Many complain they're not getting paid enough at work, but do they optimize how much money they make by working their hardest? Even those who are not in sales jobs have an opportunity to take the next step in their work by working harder towards a promotion rather than staying still in their current position. Standing still guarantees you will be in the same place years later; however, moving forward, or even attempting to, will ensure growth—externally in a better position or internally with all the experience you gained. Regardless, you will be in a better place by simply trying.

I knew I had to work much harder, but not necessarily longer. Just like many people, I didn't think I could work longer hours than I already was. I came up with a strategy that made me very successful but was actually pretty simple. I made a deal with myself that I would work hard during the forty hours I was at my job each week. I would not request overtime or extra hours; I would simply make every hour count. I frequently looked at others working, then noticed that even the best wasted so much time chatting with others, hanging out, or eating.

Years passed and this method worked wonders, but I faced a typical problem that many of you will probably relate with: My mother insisted that my education held more weight than having a $60,000 annual salary. I was 18 years old. To please my mother and avoid her any headaches on my account, I decided to listen to her and hoped for the best. After graduating high school and taking a semester off, I was forced to consider enrolling to a community college—one, because I never applied anywhere; two, because I couldn't afford anything else, while maintaining my household and three, because my grades were far from being excellent. Long story short, I had to cut back my hours and find a different job that would pay me as much as my current one, but with more structured hours.

I had no passion, I didn't like any aspect of business, and I certainly didn't know what to do, but I knew two things:

1. I liked making money

2. I enjoyed being able to be promoted.

Since my estranged father was a very successful banker, I was always intrigued by the financial industry. Perhaps it was in my blood to follow in his footsteps. Because I wanted to be successful and wealthy, I thought perhaps I would find answers there. My mother had a friend who was a manager at her local bank. She introduced me, hoping that good conversation would lead to some direction. In a matter of minutes, the bank manager was sold that, with my managerial experience and sales background, a role in banking just was a perfect fit.

I, on the other hand, wasn't sold on the idea of getting a fifty percent pay cut. The possibility of their maximum base salary, which was over $400,000, made the pay cut as the least of my concerns. My ambition of becoming a CEO turned real. I decided nonetheless to give banking a go.

Many people always ask me how I was able to get a bank management job with no education and no past banking experience. The answer is simple, but the execution, not so much.

Knowing someone who already works in the company, is single-handedly the best way to get the interview, as the human resources unit love referrals from team leaders. Since my mother had made her local bank manager a friend, she would do her best to get me through the final process with the human resources department. She was also trying to get me hired because most major organizations have a referral program that gives back to those who find qualified applicants. She would receive $5,000 if they hired me as a manager. This insight helps anyone who is applying for a job to understand the angle in which you can approach it. Any single person can develop a relationship with the team leader of their bank. Eventually approach them about working for the same company. Why wouldn't they help you, especially if there is an incentive for them—which is the case in most places—and they are confident in your skills or like your character?

The interview date was set. The time came to convince a complete stranger that, despite not having a business degree or a clue on how a bank worked, I should be hired.

This part may seem intimidating to many on the surface, but look at it from the same angle as approaching the unknown. When the unknown remains that way, the intimidation is amplified by fear rather than facts. We can peel that fear away by simply familiarizing ourselves with the concepts we don't understand, creating context and structure for the unknown by making it factual instead of emotional. We sometimes fail to understand the role of a job, simply because we are blinded with the idea of the pay. Frequently, we look at a job from the angle in which it benefits us, as opposed to how we benefit it. With that perspective, we lose our value in the mix, as we are fixated on the value the job brings to us. This is the number one reason why many people never get the job they seek, no matter how many interviews they have. The focus should always be the specific talent-based value you bring to the job, which demonstrates that you understand the value needed to get the work done. Don't simply assume your sales knowledge, for example, will be viewed an asset. That's too generic to earn real credentials. Instead, make your previous experiences relatable to the current position. For example, I understood and related my telemarketing, cold calling, and canvassing background skills to a supermarket-based banking environment because it showed value when it comes to sales experience and service. The primary goal for that particular bank I was interviewing for, located inside a supermarket, was to randomly approach people and persuade them to become banking clients. So, I figured if I could demonstrate my capabilities of cold selling or relationship building with complete strangers during the interview, I could persuade the interviewer that I possess the necessary skills to excel at the position, despite lacking a degree or direct experience in the banking industry itself. This is exactly what I did.

On my first round of interviews, I observed my environment and noticed all bankers who worked there were sitting, seemingly stuck on their computers, even though the objective was to bring clients from the aisles to the desks. This observation guided me to believe that no one was having much success. They chose to remain in their comfort zone, which was easy to recognize as I had witnessed other people doing the same thing back at my telemarketing company—and getting equally lackluster results.

Identifying this pattern allowed me to immediately demonstrate why I was a good candidate. I walked the aisles, engaging in discussion and bringing two people back to discuss their banking. I had no product knowledge, training, or idea on what the procedure was; but I understood the goal and seized the opportunity to demonstrate that my ability to adapt was the highest they had yet seen. This is the core you must understand if you work for someone else. The purpose is not to just win; the goal is to showcase your ability to adapt to what you are being asked and improve upon it, not build your own empire within someone else's space or business.

During my interview, I was also asked why I believed an 18-year-old was qualified to run a bank outlet. I responded that I didn't think I was more or less qualified than anyone else to run it; I expressed that running a bank is something anyone can learn, but growing a bank is based upon the idea of selling by doing activities that lead to transactions and not sitting behind a desk. I demonstrated in my thirty-minute interview how to actually go to the aisles of that supermarket and bring people back, the single most important activity that had yet to be executed properly by a team that had been there for over two years. I showed my worthiness based upon my actions, not relying on my resume. This helped me secure a management job in a major bank two weeks later. What I knew then was that most people can only see as far as their immediate needs and those hiring people are only looking to fulfill a necessity as well. You see, managers in the majority of organizations blame their lack of sales on short staffing as it makes it very easy to blame the lack of time for other's inability to do their job. So, it was clear by observing this manager that his biggest obstacle was looking for a way out, rather than a real solution. Since I provided both, I fulfilled his immediate need and got hired in a role much greater than what I technically qualified for on paper.

The greatest mistake one can make when looking for a job is to assume they are going to interview with a company rather than a person. As a result, people educate themselves on the company and its objectives, rather than on the person who will be interviewing them. People hire people to work for the company that they represent; the "company" doesn't hire you to work for the people who represent it. People form a company's culture and direction, and people make the hiring decisions. By understanding this, your goal becomes to subjectively appeal to the hiring person, the one you will work with and see periodically, not the "company" that will assign you an employee number and one day simply choose to delete it. I say "subjectively" because the greatest mistake one can make when looking for a job is to assume they are going to interview with a company rather than a person. As a result, people educate themselves on the company and its objectives rather than on the person who will be interviewing them. People hire people to work for the companies that they also work for; companies don't hire you to work for people

43

that who work there. The idea is to understand that the people of a company are what form a company's culture and direction, not just the company itself. By understanding this, your goal becomes to subjectively appeal to the hiring person, the one you will work with and see periodically, not the "company" that will assign you a worthless employee number and one day simply choose to delete it. I say subjectively because most people also only consider the benefits of a job before choosing to apply for a position, and yet never consciously make a decision to apply to do the work. How often do people focus on the salary, benefits, and growth opportunities rather than on the work they will be performing once hired there? Individuals worry about the destination, yet hardly the journey itself. This is typically why they remain stuck in the work and never reach further destinations when working for others. I myself looked at work very differently right from the beginning, due to my observations early on in my last company. Remember that I climbed from a telemarketer to the director of a company in three years before I was even 18 years old; and this came as the result of figuring out how to be valuable to a company, not because I wanted a promotion or was looking ahead to my future. The present is where the action takes place when you work for others, it almost guarantees your growth or failure in the future, and so I worried about the effectiveness of my work during my banking days rather than on the possibilities of the future. A big mistake many make is to focus on the opportunities coming up instead of being prepared to seize them. How often have you heard a hiring manager ask, "Where do you see yourself in five years?" only to be met with an ignorant response "as a CEO or VP." The one being interviewed thinks he or she is showing ambition while the hiring manager is wondering why someone who isn't even qualified to work in the current job they are interviewing for is already thinking of becoming a CEO. That answer qualifies the candidate as inexperienced and delusional. What good is the opportunity if you are deemed unqualified to apply?

My banking years were far from perfect. The job itself wasn't very entertaining and I was exposed to real work politics, I didn't have much experience with this in my previous job. At the bank, everything had to be done a certain way, rules couldn't be bent, and regulations played a major part of how fear was induced in employees. I had made a commitment to going to school, therefore, I needed this job, even if at the time, I believed it was short-lived. I shadowed a few people who really stood out to me, one of whom was a young 23-year-old who was already a well-established manager. I never understood why everyone praised his mediocre work. He didn't understand people, sales, or any concepts that mattered, but his customer service skills were well received. I realized then how various results played in what I would later call a *reactive* management system, one implemented by every major company out there. The point I learned was that, in order to secure your job in Corporate America, you don't have to excel; you only have to be as good as the guy who controls the problem of the week. Most managers I interacted with in Corporate America were pathetic; they had no backbone. The few that did still pretended to be puny so that no one asks more of them. I couldn't understand for the life of me why no one was actively trying to fix easy problems the company had. It just didn't make sense since so many issues could be fixed overnight, yet everyone chose to ignore the signals. For example, one problem was that due to short staffing issues, most employees would not get a chance to complete training.

Yet no one would create a geographic eco-system that allowed nearby locations to help staffing to prevent employees from missing half of their training. Instead, the managers waited until enough of their employees fell behind on training and, as a result, showed up on a company report as "incomplete" before they would send the bare minimum to training. So, the report showed less than 30% of their employees as incomplete, which by company standard, was a victory. *Bureaucratic checkbox to fix*

In Corporate America, <u>no one fixes problems</u>. Everyone simply finds a way to not appear as one. Can you imagine if your goal was to never fix a problem in your business, but rather just adjust its appearance so no one knew you had one? You would be considered insane in your own company to behave that way, but in Corporate America, it is the exact opposite—especially in banking. I noticed that those people who kept bringing up company-wide issues that were being *Same @* ignored by corporate were simply dismissed as "one who *core* doesn't play ball". This realization became the biggest lesson of my career in banking, one that would allow me to be promoted every six months for the following four years, one of which was a promotion that came with, a 72% salary increase. I never shared with people how I got this raise. I had considered it to be unwarranted, but later realized it was a perfectly executed plan with something very few of us had back then—<u>a fearless attitude.</u>

After the constant pursuit of executing sales goals and proving my ability to do the job, I came up with proactive and creative plans that showed I was working toward any goals that I had fallen short of making or any HR or service issue that plagued the company as a whole. I also had to show my strengths to the right people, such as making sure that my supervisor's boss actually knew that I had done a great job of achieving certain goals. I made sure to get "face time" with executives so they would remember my name and accomplishments. As confusing as this sounds, it was the magic formula to succeeding in Corporate America, but the worst part is that it is still the same even today.

Here is the equation:

Sales + Avoiding being on bad lists + Showcasing your results = Promotions

You may think I am joking, but I really kept this going for four years and was promoted more than eight times by just following this exact strategy. Sales-driven activities that generated revenue were always most important. So, you had to always be on top of those lists. Those other areas—like customer service issues, administrative issues or training—had their own lists, but all they consisted of were people who were either having issues or not, meaning all I had to do was just understand how the bank calculated its so called "bad lists" and make sure I didn't end up on there. If I knew that having more than three staff members not completing training looked bad, I did whatever was necessary to never have more than two. Even though it was inefficient, I wouldn't have to justify why I was not up to company standards. More importantly, my boss, who was clueless, wouldn't have to justify to his boss why I had a problem. Since no one would ever see my name on bad lists, I managed to either be first with all my sales numbers, which was almost impossible, or find a way to vocalize my sales efforts even when I completely failed to meet goals. I picked the easy way, which was to vocalize my success and hide my failures. I did simply always stepped up to share the most incredible stories about how my team and I closed businesses. I would come up with elaborate success stories that were far from the truth but very much aligned with the company's overall goals and directives. If we closed a big loan just because someone walked in and happened to choose my bank, I came up with a great story that described how our efforts with outreach calling led to closing the sale, giving everyone above me (who also used this same strategy) the ammunition they needed to look even better. What they must have known—but certainly cared less about— was that with each story I shared, they were required to tell their managers where it came from, making them always speak of me. I had major key players in the bank hearing my name daily for nothing more than perfectly executed success stories, focused on exaggerated sales stories. This is the key to getting raises and promotions in major companies. Most immediate supervisors had very little control over budgets, yet were the ones who submitted any requests up the chain, justifying it to someone who ordinarily wouldn't have heard or interacted with them. In this case, every time a request went to the top, those people heard of me. I strategically created stories to keep me ahead of all my peers and quickly was considered above my peers with every promotion and story.

This strategy earned me a lot of money as my promotions were of position, title, and increased compensation. It also made me appear to be a sales superstar, which I was to some degree but I hated being labeled with as my performance kept me stuck in sales management roles since the bank didn't want to lose the revenue. The issue became that, while I made more money, I was unfulfilled.

By then, I had already dropped out of college, recovered my 50% salary loss from when I started, and had decided that banking was my career as well as part of my purpose. I was excited about the road ahead. I learned something interesting about myself: I was a good teacher to my staff. No matter who had worked for me, I never had those issues that other managers had experienced in their office, caused by their so-called "bad employees". I always attracted top talent and had loyalty, even when I did very little to earn it. I started paying attention to this unique skill, as I felt that, with some work, it could become a talent. Little did I know then that this would become my greatest strength and the birth of my purpose.

The 3 Rule Leaders

The key to my success in leading others in banking could be summed up in the greatest, yet simplest leadership traits.

1. **Be fair:** The biggest mistake managers make when attempting to be leaders is to think that they must be sweet, sympathetic, and nice to be liked by their workers. The reality is that being nice is not directly correlated with being a good leader. Being a jerk is not necessary either as leading through fear is something that tends to give good short-term results, but certainly not long-term growth. The idea of being fair is no different than saying "be balanced" and allows you to create the perfect guideline that brings productivity and personal growth together. By being fair, you force the individual to grow internally, learn, and get better, while making sure the objectives are reached and goals met.

    While there are times you may not find yourself on the nicer side of a conversation, you will discover that being harsh but fair with people will lead them to not hold disagreements or your criticism of their work against you because they'll know your feedback is not out in left field, but rather communicated consistently, in a progressive manner and for their very own benefit. The key is the consistency in your message. For instance, a nice manager would want to grant every request for a day off he can, if scheduling permits. A fair manager would gauge if the objectives are on track, they have been met from the individual and then make a decision as to whether to grant the request or not. While some may consider the reason for the request, I wouldn't. Being fair includes being fair to yourself, the objectives, and the team. This requires you to be unemotional and logical in your approach.

The difference in this situation of being looked at as a jerk is the communication aspect. Are you saying, "no", or are you justifying your "no" so that it can be a learning experience for growth? Either way, look at leadership from a "being fair" perspective rather than just being nice.

2. **Raise your standards:** I never shared the same standards for my team that my corporation held for its employees. I always said that being the best of the average group made you the worst of the best. My standards always exceeded the company's, and the training I provided was better and more extensive than the one I was given to use. I understood what it took to be successful within each role and designed my own training programs to support my high expectations.

Correct Expectations + Quality Training + Fair Support = New Team/Family Member

Company Expectations + Training + Being nice or a dick = Employee

Most expectations that come from the top of an organization are typically focused on the minimum people that are required to keep their roles. This limiting belief didn't help people get promoted or advance in their skills, so raising my standards meant that even if we fell short twenty percent, my teams was always ahead. High expectations are a great way to lead, but also require the support needed to ensure it is reasonable and possible for team members to meet those elevated expectations. If one relies on the corporate training model but has much higher expectations, then the team will typically fail. In addition, incredible training coupled with lower expectations means the team members themselves will not advance and eventually find themselves bored and unmotivated, and they will find a more challenging opportunity. The goal is to match the level of expectations with the level of support and the level of training. Therefore, you empower anyone to do any task since you are taking ownership of their training just as much as you expect them to take ownership of your expectations. This dynamic indirectly creates a mentee-mentor situation that works well both in Corporate America as well as small business ownership. I was always known as the toughest manager to work for, partly because I fired more people and my expectations were higher than anyone else. However, I also had the highest and fastest track record of promoting people. You can't have one without the other and be considered effective. If you fire too many people and don't promote more people, then it is your training that is flawed; if it's the opposite, then you are typically not meeting goals. The idea is to find a balance. Set your sights high and collectively meet the needs of those around you while pushing everyone else up to the next phase.

3. **Own your word:** In business, just as much as in leadership, your word holds more weight than you might imagine. Most people today meet people expecting their best, meaning you almost have their trust from the very first moment you meet them, but it is then your obligation to work hard to retain the trust. While you may ask yourself why you would even care, I like to think of it as an investment in the team member you are nurturing and who will contribute heavily to your success. My track record of firing and hiring people followed me everywhere and, in many cases, was frowned up by my human resources

department. I didn't care about the rules because no one understood how I was able to hire and fire people left and right. and it all came down to holding my word. Regardless that I spoke to someone about their mid-year review or if I mentioned a follow-up in a week, setting expectations so that employees didn't end up on corrective action was what mattered. I followed through the exact same way I originally stated. If I promised someone a promotion based on a set of baselines they had to reach, I would promote them when they met those parameters, even if my boss disagreed. I would go as far as promoting them in another company elsewhere outside of the company they worked in. If I told someone that not doing their job would lead to their termination on that Monday, I would follow through with my promise on Monday if they hadn't stepped up to improve. No matter what I said, I would live up to it and there lied my greatest weapon: My ability to use my words as the roadmap to success and to never be questioned about my commitment to follow through on it. This differentiated my career from my peers, both from my boss's standpoint as well as my employees. The idea was that promises made were promises kept, even when it came down to goals, or expectations others had of me. This leadership trait was also one of the most important entrepreneurial lessons of my life as I understood how important holding my word was even to myself. If I promised myself a Lamborghini by the time I turned 24 years old, I had to get one by then. Alternative options did not exist, because if I broke any of my own goals, I would have to keep my mouth shut. Promises made to myself held the highest impact on my own life, so under no circumstance could they ever be broken. This became my motto and part of the reason my life accelerated much faster, and perchance too fast as my corporate career ended abruptly at the age of 25.

Lost Purpose

After seven years in banking, I was getting bored. Just like many out there, I was constantly looking for more. The thirst for more resulted in making a mistake that led to my termination from banking—for a mistake that even my boss said didn't warrant the punishment. Nonetheless, a mistake cost me my job. After allowing my super-ego take control and cost my banking career, a bizarre yet necessary thing happened to me. I lost my purpose and my main reason to be pushing my own boundaries and limitations.

It is interesting how things play out. All I knew was how to be a leader, banker, manager, among other titles. The person I looked up to, someone whom I believed in, took this title away from me. After having worked for seven years, I was dismissed with a "we don't value you anymore" because of one mistake. I felt betrayed and lost; I didn't know what to do. I spent weeks sitting at a coffee shop near a shopping center in my town, wondering to myself what I would do next. It had no relation to money as I was financially secure, based on great investments I had made and a side business I had. It wasn't that I didn't know what else to do, but I didn't want to do anything else. I wasted thirty days staring at my Lamborghini while sitting at that coffee shop. I even held onto Alan Greenspan's book. I had only managed to read the first three pages over and over, each day not remembering what I read the day before. I knew then that nothing I had ever done in life held any weight as it was always done within the four walls of someone else's imagination and passion. I was only playing a minor role in someone else's business. While I felt important because those around me fed me stuff to make me more effective, I realized that my importance was glorified by my own view of it. I comprehended something incredible about my whole career that put me back on track almost instantly.

A New View on Corporate America

I understood I had scammed myself by misunderstanding what Corporate America was and what loyalty really meant. I was working for others. I was building their dreams. I was loyal to my boss, loyal to my employees, and loyal to my company. The constant reminders from people, books, and media outlets talked of being cautious when it came to building other people's dreams and I fell victim of the greatest scam on earth. I should have known better.

NOT AT ALL! The biggest scam was that I believed in that garbage and that's why I was hurt. I had the wrong perspective on why I worked for others and I had found purpose in something that I never really understood. I bought into the idea that I was building someone else's empire when, in reality, I was doing anything but that. I was getting paid the entire time I went to work and, while it may have looked like I was actually helping a corporation become richer and more effective through the job I had, what I was really doing was making as much money as I could as fast as I could, improving my very own life.

It was easier to blame my failure on the idea that the American dream was dead rather than on the fact that I was selfish and had never really looked for my purpose. I had sold out for a financially secure life. I learned that what I was doing these past seven years was only built around myself. I always was doing nothing more than building and bridging my own life. I had consciously exchanged my time for money. I had learned skills that I could forever use. I discovered a passion for helping others that no title could take away and, more importantly, I overcame many fears that I can today use to succeed. Thus, perhaps my loyalty was always to myself and this was why Corporate America never had any loyalty to me in exchange.

If someone would have offered me twice the money, I would have been gone; conversely, if my boss could have replaced me for half the money, I would have also been gone, which in this case, became real. So, at the end, is there anyone who was cheated? Not actually. By admitting that I misunderstood what happened to me, I realized that no one really took this away from me. I chose to give it up and, therefore, I was losing time by not allowing the process to take its place. In other words, I was not allowing this door to close. Instead I was holding on to the idea that I could possibly go back and start to work in Corporate America again. I did not want anything to do with building another company's empire in exchange for money, so I decided to close that door and move forward immediately.

The Birth of VIP

As I stated earlier, making money at a young age leaves you with a very good taste in your mouth, especially if it is done so legally. As an immigrant 15 year-old without a green card, I leveraged my two immigrant friends into helping me create a side car wash business. I originally wanted to bring them to work alongside me in the office, but the risk of being discovered as not having a green card was greater than the reward. During my workdays, I had a fifteen-minute break that was spent going to the local arcade playing video games. One day I noticed a van cleaning cars in the parking lot. I engaged in a small conversation with the employee that resulted in an interesting idea, one that would become a forty million business be exact. I decided to start a mobile car wash business in that very same office complex, which housed around one thousand residents and over three hundred businesses. I knew that there would be enough work to keep me busy all year and I since liked cleaning cars, did not mind at all. Immediately, flyers were printed with my brick-size cell number on them (yes this was when they first introduced cell phones and I had a giant Nokia hanging on my waist lol), and over five hundred flyers were distributed a week. After three months I did not receive one single call. Before and after my shifts at my telemarketing work, I would go out in the parking lot to pick up any flyers that were thrown on the floor. I did this almost every day and on the fourth month, I finally received a call that my very first client wanted a wash and wax. It was a white 1991 300ZX turbo, a car that in that time was still very well respected. It needed some heavy work, but after five hours it looked new again. I was in high school full time and worked five hours per day every day after school including a twelve-hour shift on Saturdays and Sundays, which made it almost impossible for me to do the car wash work to that extent on a daily basis. To avoid rejecting customers, I decided hire one of my immigrant high school friend who had no work and offered to pay him $20 to do the work while I was in the office working my regular job. I would schedule the job and he would wash and detail each car to perfection using the finest wax from the local auto store. After realizing how tedious and much work there was, I decided to leave my unemployed friend and his buddy in charge of all cleanings and detailing, as there was simply no way I could commit to high school, a full time job and this new business. As more calls came in, we decreased the price to wash cars to ten dollars, detail them for $100; and even began to fix small maintenance requests as I mentioned earlier. All of this was done while I was still working daily as a telemarketer in one of those very same offices; no one at work knew my involvement and everyone used my services. Two years passed, and by my 17th birthday, we grew to $150,000 in annual revenue, which mainly was compensation for my co-workers and very little was left for me. What mattered was continuity and momentum, not profit. I always knew that keeping the flow going was key, even if at the time, I had no way to capitalize on this personally. I wanted to own a business and I did, and the money would later manifest itself.

Nonetheless, our process was non-existent, our methods inefficient, our expenses high, and our labor force illegal— but it didn't stop us from continuing forward. Eventually, we started getting busier and I was getting less interested in the business; I was more focused on my career as a manager in the remodeling world, which was going quite well. As more time went by, I would actually concentrate more on bringing revenue for this company I worked for and less for my own car wash business. I was young and confused as I thought that washing cars didn't have a prestigious feel to it like being called a "manager". The business continued without me and operations were handled by my two friends who were running it full-time. I eventually even stopped getting paid, as we really didn't have any formal agreement of any sort. We hadn't even discussed what we each wanted out of the company. He worked and got paid, and I slowly drifted away and disappeared in the background, as I decided to take my focus elsewhere. My day job eventually moved away and into banking and I lost interest all together. I gave up on car washes, or so I thought.

Years passed and my banking career had started. I hated my job early on but I pushed forward focusing not on the situation but the work. If I was going to spend ten hours at work, it only made sense that I maximize my impact and productivity while there. One day a client walked in and impressed me as someone I should know. His name was Richard and he was a developer who built homes under the umbrella of Ryan Homes and Toll Brothers, two homebuilding companies that were popping up everywhere. One discussion with him, and I was intrigued about the idea of buying land, and selling the property to bigger companies that wanted to build homes there.

In twenty minutes, he explained what, at the time, I believed to be a joke because I didn't understand how something so easy was not being done by everyone else. I asked multiple questions to learn more. Right after, I conversed with my uncle Parviz, who had helped me buy my first home when I had turned 18, about the possibility of pursuing this niche in real estate. I had a great income and disposable money, so it made sense to take a look at my options to buy my first piece of land.

Long story short, my ambition outweighed my capacity and six months later, I was still looking for land with no break in sight. Even though the information Richard had given me was relevant, his connections in the industry were more important in order for me to successfully duplicate his footsteps. He had more than ten years on me in the industry and, at this point, I had nothing. Because I was ready to give up, I decided to attempt to make such connections. A Ryan Homes development had a sales office a mile down the road from where I lived. I planned to walk in hoping to find a good contact that could bridge my lack of connection in the business. To my surprise, the sales representative was even more confused than me and had absolutely no idea what I was talking about. He seemed very interested in what I was saying that I wasn't even sure if it was a good idea to share all the details as Richard had shared with me. I chose to move on, but as I was walking out, I saw a line of people waiting to chat with the same person I was talking with and couldn't understand why. As ignorant as I was, I assumed everyone was there to inquire information that I already knew: there were no homes were for sale. I was intrigued; hence, I stayed to speak with the crowd; then I learned an essential fact that would change my life forever.

The Quick Real Estate Side Play

I discovered that everyone there was waiting to buy a home early, a year early to be exact—not only to get it at a great deal, but also because they wanted to guarantee they got one of these new homes, as inventory in this region was scarce. This got me wondering, "Why would anyone not be guaranteed a home when they have money to buy one?"

I couldn't figure this out for week, but eventually I introduced myself to the idea of supply and demand, and the simple correlation with price. I learned how the price swings one way or the other, depending on the level of supply and demand. I became equally fascinated with this new concept as my initial one of buying land and selling it. This one seemed simpler as all I had to do was buy homes early and sell them later for more money. Because I assumed that each home would require a massive ten percent deposit to lock down a home, I put my cash together, knowing the risk was worth the attempt and moved forward to purchase my first investment pre-construction home.

To my surprise, each home didn't require ten percent down but rather a down payment of five to ten thousand dollars. Because these pre-construction homes were purchased so early, the builder could not yet provide any firm pricing information on options until the delivery was set in stone, but would guarantee the purchase price itself of the home, and more importantly, guarantee the lot location you selected.

Side note: If every path to success were as simple as doing the work, many people would be very rich today; but it is much more than that. It is about adapting and creating momentum while doing the work as the path to success in most unsuccessful people's head is as simple as:

Start to Finish

For people who have been in business, the equation reads quite differently.

Thought of starting -> Preparation -> Gaining skills -> or Doing other jobs that help you create stability -> Starting -> Finishing

The path to the starting line is one that is much more difficult than the path from start to finish.

End of Side Note

Going back to my story. When I started buying lots, I understood the power of flipping things based on the idea of supply and demand. I joined the line for every single home site within a one-hundred-mile RADIUS of my own house in northern Virginia, and would wait in line to buy a lot. I even asked if new communities were planned in six months and where they would be going up by the same builder. I marked sites before they were announced and randomly drove by to see when sales offices were built so that I could be first in line. Once a lot was purchased, I had a total of seven to eleven months to resell my allocation before I was forced to actually purchase the home itself. The best part was that the financial capacity to purchase a home had to be provided at each securing of a lot, but because none of these homes would end up actually bought, they would not be reported on my credit. The power here was that I was able to buy ten to fifteen lots using a bank approval letter (which was pretty easy to secure since I worked in a high leadership position in a major bank). The biggest obstacle I faced was how to sell the houses since I didn't technically own them yet. The conservative approach would have been to take ownership and then sell them conventionally, but that wouldn't have been that easy as the loan process coupled with picking expensive options can add up quickly especially when buying many homes. I decided the best time to sell was before the home was built, about 30 days before options were to be picked, allowing anyone to select their home as they want it with a much cheaper base price. During the six months I held the allocation, more and more homes were sold, some as low priced as mine while others with premiums based on how much demand there was and how limited the supplies were. Premiums would range from $30,000 to $150,000, all depending on the price of the house. By the time the six months had passed, every lot I had purchased had an average premium of over $50,000. That meant that the base price was now $50,000 dollars higher than when I purchased the lot, and people would have to wait even longer to get their homes as they were still facing the same six-month wait I had already faced. This was a great opportunity because I could bridge the time lost and get people a cheaper home without having to advertise what I was selling, since I had a line of clients waiting for me. People were eager to buy homes, pay more for them, and even wait six months, if necessary. I leveraged this concept by engaging people who were waiting in line by waiting with them and getting to know which was a better fit for taking over my particular acquisition. I offered my premiums at $10,000 under the builder's and offered a better lot that would be ready earlier. Even though I was still a full-time bank manager, I went to the sales office every day from 7:00 a.m. to 9:00 a.m., because in the mornings, I could find a better crowd that could not resist the value. Early people usually showed more interest and willingness to buy immediately, versus those just inquiring at any time in the day. So, every morning I waited in line, I sold a lot and made between $40,000 and $50,000. I replicated this process 72 times before the local builders started grasping a pattern and put an end to this elaborate way to flip homes. I became the middle man in an industry that truly didn't have a need for one.

The Rebirth of VIP

Being a middle man in a transaction and learning the skills that came along it gave birth to the *VIP Motoring* brand. What if I could buy exotic cars much cheaper than they are worth, hold them and resell them later? I thought of applying the same concepts to exotic cars—of buying right, holding the asset, and reselling it later. I compiled a list of all the things I would need, such as great connections with car dealerships, allocations on new cars with high demand and low supply, and lots of capital, which I had just gained.

But let's not get too far ahead yet. While VIP was detailing cars, and making good side money for two people, the model was far from a business and was very labor intensive. As I grew in Corporate America, my love for cars and higher salary allowed me to buy some pretty nice cars, such as a 911 Turbo by Gemballa, followed by a 2004 Lamborghini Gallardo. All cars were modified and, at the time, no one in my northern Virginia region was focusing their efforts on customizing high-end exotic cars. I decided just from a hobby standpoint to customize mine, which always brought in many questions by other local car owners like, "Who did the work?" I would answer them by telling them that my own small repair company had done the work, even though I was not fully involved in VIP because it was in its early stages and still nothing more than that same old car wash company. I went back to make a proposal to my same old friends who had not really scaled the business any further than where I had left it. We agreed to re-launch the business as a legal entity and name it VIP Motoring. With more and more people interested, I decided to start selling wheels, suspension, and minor upgrades for exotic cars, instead of just washing all types of cars. We moved into a small warehouse and started changing our focus.

Far from an operation and much more aligned to a good hustle, my work caught the attention of a local Ferrari dealer who wanted to offer its clients better performance options for their cars straight from the factory. Higher upsells, the ability to finance parts with the cars, and a one-stop shop rather than having people seek alternatives like mine...fast forward 90 days of discussion and a partnership was formed to provide wheels and carbon fiber parts to a very niche market, directly at the dealership on a net-45 basis (giving them 45 days to sell the parts rather than paying upfront). Word got out and after six months of successful collaboration, another four exotic car dealerships within a 100-mile RADIUS that were not competing with that Ferrari dealer joined our network. I had the four most dominant local dealerships selling parts I provided them or white labeled from other tuners and manufacturers, direct to their consumers with very little effort as the economy was booming. People could finance 130% of their cars without effort or red tape from banks.

After successfully incurring revenue for twenty-four months, a financial storm started brewing, that involved what is known today as "the great recession." The days of financing exotic cars for 130% with no money down, or financing the extra accessories you wanted, were now gone. If I had learned anything in my experience in real estate, it was the importance of buying when demand is low, and supply high and reselling in the opposite financial climate. It was time to buy lots of leftover exotic cars from dealers who couldn't sell their cars, no matter how in demand they were six months ago. I had accumulated the right amount of money to make purchases, but the reality was that no business without revenue can survive, and my strategy was flawed. It was focused on buying these luxury cars, not yet reselling them, as the recession was certainly going to last longer than six months. Without revenue, holding assets for all my cash worth may not be the best idea, especially when the risk always existed that my prediction was wrong and that my original idea would be useless if the recession didn't end or the damage from it would be more. While it was a great idea, it was far from perfect.

Once again bridging the problem became the goal and, as a result, VIP Motoring was born, the world's first exotic car investment company. You, as a client, no longer needed to insure, register, or pay taxes on this alternative investment opportunity. What better than a guaranteed principal, high possible return, and the exact opposite pattern as other investment opportunities that were conventional like real estate or the stock market? I allowed people to share the cost of holding assets in exchange for use, managing the asset for both a fee, consulting advice, and the management of the process for a percent of the gains. Using my finance background and long list of wealthy clients who had supported me during my banking days now long behind me, I was able to spend my own $1.6 million in depreciated automotive investments and pass the assets on to new clients who all were eager to try this new strategy. They invested their trust in me since the methodology didn't have long-term proof behind it. After unloading my own inventory on clients and buying new inventory with my new-found liquidity, I quickly brought in over $20 million in investor capital to fund inventory that could sit there over the course of the next three years possibly.

Within three years, I restructured the company to go from a small repair workshop that sold wheels and body kits, to one of the largest concierge services in the United States on the basis of growth revenue.

The investment into VIP Motoring only came as the necessity to find my purpose once my banking days were behind me. Its growth, however, was based on two very simple principles that have been followed in every single new business founded since then.

The New Scaling Approach

The key to scaling a business isn't to sell more but to find a way to recycle customers or resources, which I will break down in detail for you later in this book. Every single business out there accumulates these two things, no matter how small or how big they get. The key is to create verticals using those two specific guidelines. For instance, if affluent exotic car buyers are usually watch buyers, then having a list of such clients means you could sell them watches, too. Resources like a storage facility to maintain those car-based investments we discussed, or a staff of accountants could lead to new services like actually offering accounting services, storage space, or even brokering car deals that may not be a fit for investment purposes.

The key isn't to become a "do it all" service, but rather to do the things for which you already have demand (customers), or the ability to fulfill without the extra work (resources). This allowed us to scale from one million dollars or so in revenue from services over three million dollars by selling high-end timepieces, accounting advice, and brokering services like luxury vacations, cars and art—all while we waited for those investments in rare exotic inventory to pay back their dividends.

VIP Motoring was formed when I had just turned 15 years old. It took ten years of absentee ownership to learn skills that, at the time, were considered irrelevant, only to come back to the realization of its capacity. It took another four years of dedicated hard work after that with my own funding that was connected on two different occasions by doing other things that are somewhat unrelated. Also, I leveraged other people's fear of the end of the current economy as we knew it to create a unique opportunity for myself. To date, VIP Motoring operates out of Virginia and Florida, and has reached peaks of revenue over $40 million annually continuously being a profitable business even though I no longer need to manage it daily.

The Three-Million-Dollar Failure of Secret Consulting

Let's go back to that time when I was fired from my Corporate America job. Although the automotive and luxury industry appeal to me enough to give VIP Motoring the attention it deserves, the idea of my passion project also started to take shape then, but with a big road block. During my corporate career, one of the most rewarding aspects of my job was training and growing talent. During six months of my time working in finance, I also headed the entire training department for sales and service training. I helped create many training programs that would teach bankers how to be more efficient with closing their sales in various environments, like specialty branches, supermarkets, and networking events. I also created a few service models that would help reshape the way people see and think of being of service to others, especially in an industry as greedy as banking.

When I was terminated from my role as vice president in banking, I took with me all the training I had accumulated but had yet to launch. I ended up leaving with the intention of creating and selling a training program, with all the good practices and successful actions, to competing banks, out of anger and regret. In 2006, I started a company called Secret Consulting where I would secretly help major businesses that were in need of training for a low fee. This idea, after twelve months of relentless pushing to sell my services, failed miserably.

In December 2008, I received a call from a prospect who had been a follower of my blog, and who wanted to retain my services to help him scale an online business. While far from my area of expertise, it seemed at the time to be my only shot at actually creating any type of revenue for this now dying company. While my original plan to help young people was not playing out as I expected, I was also now in a unique position to adapt to what the market was telling me was needed. With this new client, who retained our services for 12 months, came the need to scale a new team in this vertical, one that will later become the essential reason why the Secret Entourage blog would succeed to break its own seven figures. The team I scaled consisted of a designer, coder, programmer, marketer, and myself, as a copywriter in the earlier stages. Together, we formed a small but very effective marketing company that became the core of what Secret Consulting was, a digital marketing company for lifestyle businesses that we would scale to a reasonable, but profitable two million dollars in annual revenue

Although the core of Secret Consulting was a failure, the product that came out of it was not only profitable but also gave the opportunity for the rebirth of its failed blog. When I started to build SecretConsulting.com, I had no visitors, followers, or revenue. Nonetheless, the exchange for my effort was my very first client who would not have been able to find me without that same blog, as well as the foundational team that would convert the blog to the business of Secret Entourage.

My passion comes from helping educate and grow talent, and yet none of my businesses aligning with this core talent of mine. Secret Consulting took the shape of a hobby and the need to venture in a very different direction. I wanted to be in the Internet marketing space for two core reasons: the ability to scale with minimal overhead, and the opportunity to recycle resources faster and more efficiently than any other business.

So, I used my passion to embark on yet a new chapter in my life by changing Secret Consulting to Secret Entourage. I entered into the online marketing space with a whole new approach.

The Five Years of Informal Education

Secret Consulting was a failed revenge attempt as my original intention was to sell my knowledge to the competitors of that same corporate job I was let go from. Within that anger lay a silver lining. Part of this business focused on maintaining a blog that coached and helped others find their way, while the other focused on selling leadership and service programs to major companies. I did not have experience in this space and, the truth was, I didn't know what I was doing on many levels. I was not only confused on how to grow the business, but I didn't even understand what business I was in.

After twelve months of scrambling, calling on clients, and updating a blog, I realized how lost I really was. Still, there was this very deep, inner belief that a road would manifest itself eventually. In my head, I was simply laying stones to allow me to move forward, hoping that with each step, I would gain a vision that would guide me to the next one. I took many steps in many directions and found myself equally lost a year later.

The reality was that each step forward came from an emotional reaction, rather than a strategic one. I decided then that even though I had no clue what I was doing, nor any idea what direction I would take, I knew inside my heart that my Secret Consulting business ideas were both good. Nevertheless, my two businesses did not have the same targets, and so I decided that while I still believed in both, they were not meant to grow in the same direction and co-exist.

Consequently, I decided to separate the two to prevent my confused emotional misguidance from driving the faith of both companies into the ground. I had, after all, failed for one full year, attempting to bring together a business that simply was built on anger. From this decision came the birth of two companies: Secret Entourage, the motivational website, and Secret Consulting, the branding, leadership, management consulting company. Both lacked revenue and clients, which became the single greatest decision and greatest challenge I would ever face. Two companies in different industries in which I had no experience, resources, understanding, or team—just the sheer desire to succeed with no data or fact that backed any of my decisions.

Secret Consulting would go on to yet become one more business, one that focused on getting clients, completing work, and getting paid. I shifted its direction many times until I eventually focused the core of its day-to-day activities to becoming a full digital branding agency that served Fortune 500 companies. I steered it not so much in its existing ideology of training companies' employees, but instead guided the business to becoming their branding arm. Secret Consulting ran parallel to Secret Entourage, an online brand that, in itself, was becoming a true reflection of what all these different people I had brought together on my team were capable of doing. Every one of the employees I had used to help build the ultimate motivation site was "recycled"; I leveraged their talents to build other brands that were becoming clients of Secret Consulting. This was not only influencing the employee base to create a new vertical of revenue, but it was keeping them paid, as Secret Entourage wasn't really in a place to be able to pay them normal salaries or compensation for their work. In other words, the two companies fed one another in revenue and resources until they each stood on their own.

Sheer Force, Not Money-based Growth

Why didn't I just pay to grow both companies? A question I get asked quite often was why wouldn't I invest my own money in my two companies. The answer is simple: I didn't know how to. I knew early on that both companies were experimental and I understood that both companies would require tons of work and effort, but what I didn't understand then was how either company would ever make me any money. This was the missing ingredient as I was venturing into an industry I didn't know or comprehend.

So, I exchanged my own monetary injection for a lot of sweat equity that would clarify my vision and the path the companies should be taking. I recognized that I didn't understand the concept enough to invest in it—even though I was leading it. I didn't want any infusion of cash to become a buffer. I wanted to know if these companies—like my existing one, VIP Motoring—could fund themselves to a level of efficiency. Then without fear, I would inject the company with even more cash of my own. I needed to prove it to myself and so I decided to grow the brand by doing what I did best. I leveraged my greatest ability, which was managing people and fostering talent, as the core driver of the direction I took in the business. I found a marketer, named Alan Dang, who was a recent high school graduate with a passion for cars. He was highly unmotivated, but possessed an intricate understanding of the online marketing world. I also found Navid Norouzi, a highly talented programmer and designer who had played it safe his whole life, focusing on a conventional and formal growth process. As a result, I decided to create a company whose core methodology of helping people would be fueled and driven by my ability to grow these two people into the professionals they needed to become in order to bring to life this grand idea of reshaping the motivation and education world for Generation Y.

The team dynamic was quite bizarre and unlikely to work out because Alan was unmotivated due to his young age, and Navid was unable to multitask because his background was in a formalized corporate IT job. Everyone also had their own ideas of what the website should look like and what our roles should be. We were all different. We didn't understand what the other did. All three of us also brought very different experience levels, motivations, maturity, and financial backing, which again amplified this idea that failure was imminent.

The first two years were a disaster since we were creating content no one wanted to read, designing a brand people considered unattractive, misunderstanding our own revenue model, and being very misaligned in terms of vision. The path was foggy and the amount of work was constantly increasing, as were the challenges that arose from not understanding the destination or milestones we needed to accomplish to get there. Every direction we took was met with early opposition and forced us to change course, once again creating more work for us, while we remained in the exact same place as when we started. It was as if we were a three-headed dragon: three minds sharing the singular body of Secret Entourage. We were all conjoined with the business. Yet each of us was heading in a separate direction, pulling away, only to be held back by the other.

Despite our very different work ethics, misguidance, dissimilarities, and confusion; we shared two things that allowed us to break through and take a simple idea to $40,000 in annual revenue: trust and awareness. We trusted one another; plus, we were very cautious to not create any reasons to betray that trust. Our awareness enabled us to overcome our differences. We still didn't see eye to eye, but comprehended in a common fashion what needed to be done and what role we had committed to play. In our third year, we created revenue by introducing products, ranging from e-books to basic how-to guides, all sold for very small prices. While $40,000 a year wasn't enough to pay anyone, hire more staff or even an amount to be proud of, it proved that we now had a basis for a revenue model. The key to staying on track was the *handcuff strategy* I used to prevent both Alan and Navid from being able to leave or look elsewhere.

> The *handcuff strategy*: Creating a business model or reason that someone cannot voluntarily leave the business. This strategy is based on having too much time, money, or sweat equity invested so that it is difficult to leave the business. You do this by unveiling small glimpses of victory and vision so that you make the fear of leaving at the cost of losing on the upside the primary reason why no one leaves.

While this strategy successfully pushed them to work hard, and prevented them from moving on to more lucrative projects, it afforded me the opportunity to explore more ways for this project to gain strong traction.

I finally figured out four essential components of a set order that would change the course of Secret Entourage forever.

1. **Real photography:** Most website and marketing pictures were focused on stock photography rather than real and current innovative, artistic photography. We decided to leverage our existing photography resources to bring together a unique visual experience. At VIP Motoring, I worked with some talented automotive photographers who were friends of my brands and willing to help. I asked if they would mind if I used their photographs in my designs and they readily

agreed. At the time, no one was leveraging photography the way we were due to lack of access to amazingly beautiful photo work.

2. **Separate design from coding:** I rapidly realized that programming and design do not go hand in hand. I separated the design work of our brand from the implementation. I discovered that programmers think in limitation and artists think with their imagination. To ask a programmer to design and code a website meant having to accept that every design I would receive would be limited to the depth of their capacity to implement such design. I wanted ground-breaking designs, so I looked at those photographers who were doing photo work and asked one of them in particular to redesign just our home page. Since photographers already use Photoshop all day, it made sense to reach out to one to redesign the possibilities of my brand. The photographer brought the image I had always envisioned to life. The fog blocking my vision started to clear and direction made more sense. I finally had in front of me the beginning of a brand that looked exactly as I expected it to. I expected this shift in direction would show me the difference between limitations and imagination, and I wasn't disappointed.

3. **Reinvent an old trick:** The third step meant figuring out an edge in bringing traffic or customers, as you would call them in a conventional business. Using that same photo component, we decided to recreate the idea of what motivational quotes should look like. Keep in mind that this was before Instagram was even created and before it was used as a motivational tool. At a time when the coolest motivational quote online was using a stock photo of two people holding hands, we re-invented the entire concept of motivational quotes by

using the greatest and most beautiful automotive photography of the latest luxury lifestyle components without any costs. The success came from the pure basis of great partnerships and shared resources between a business that fed them work and a new brand that gave them exposure. And so, we generated massive interest on social media, and pivoted towards the rise of Instagram, as the photo-based social experience made perfect sense for us. Our entire brand had shifted towards beautiful imagery and we now had the perfect platform to do it on. This shift took us from $40,000 the year before to $450,000 in revenue in our second year.

4. **Realize we were never an online company:** While our brand was online, so was our ability to reach people. However, we soon realized that we weren't an online company. As a matter of fact, the business represented a social movement with an online connection hub. We enlightened people who weren't on Google and got them to experience a whole new level of self-education. We understood that SEO and Google ads wouldn't reach our clients; they would be on social media instead. Our target demographic was online searching for resources; they were chilling at home, browsing their phones to stay in touch with their friends, family and just to see what is going on. This revelation halted most of the Internet-centered efforts and instead focus on how to get in front of more social people.

The Birth of a Theory

When I originally started Secret Entourage, I didn't understand why anyone would want to hear the knowledge that I had to sell. It was, after all, information that was readily available on the Internet. Our audience didn't realize that truth. However, it didn't help that I couldn't figure out how to differentiate Secret Entourage from hundreds of other websites that were also teaching basic business and leadership concepts.

During my banking career, my greatest ability was fostering other people's talent and teaching them the basic awareness necessary to succeed in business and in life. Every time I would coach someone, I showed a drawing of three circles on three post-it notes explaining to them that their success lied outside of their comfort zone and their ability to see past themselves. It was always this particular talk that would trigger a need for greatness within the people I coached. During one of my coaching sessions with a member of the Secret Entourage team, I used the same three-circle methodology on paper. A few strokes of pen that day made me realize what Secret Entourage was missing all these years was a process or system that was exclusive to it. The business needed a personality, something to stand for and on. Thus came the seven-month journey to writing *Third Circle Theory: Purpose through Observation*. This book would not only bridge the gap between dreaming and taking action for over 200,000 people who have read it to date, but also validate the authenticity and power of Secret Entourage as a legitimate source of entrepreneur education.

Bringing It All Together

Third Circle Theory became a bestseller, leveraging the same strategy that Secret Entourage had used to grow to date, which was a robust social media campaign focused on reaching the ideal demographic. The best part of this book's achievement was that every copy sold led to more interest in Secret Entourage and ended up giving us the additional boost we needed to be noticed.

While my ability to teach people on Secret Entourage was fantastic, it was misunderstood by many as we mixed lifestyle and business. Many companies had previously tried this concept but royally failed due to poor execution. The principle didn't resonate well with more established entrepreneurs but worked well for younger ones. *Third Circle Theory* showed our real intentions, and the list of accredited entrepreneurs demonstrated that Secret Entourage possessed much more substance than just any other business site. It would help bring back and reshape the true meaning of entrepreneurship. With more and more entrepreneurs endorsing the book and being willing to talk to us, the family would expand and so would our reach and our revenue.

The Ultimate Bet

Selling *Third Circle Theory* as a single book wasn't enough to help us grow and sustain past the seven-figure mark. Consequently, we had to come up with creative ways to generate more revenue to survive and grow. The idea of bundling the book came shortly after and we decided to sell an entire collection of e-books and courses for $97. While the book was growing in popularity, I had written eight other e-books that, together with *Third Circle* Theory, would create the perfect framework. Prior to *Third Circle Theory*, those were the same books that had helped us create a revenue model for Secret Entourage. With this bundle, we created a more relevant product.

Next, we developed the unique marketing proposition to help sell it. I offered everyone the opportunity to receive a 200% money-back guarantee when we launched the bundle. I was so confident that *Third Circle Theory* would change everything that I bet a lot of my own personal money on it. With sales in the six digits in volume, each and every day meant that I could lose massive amounts of money if I had to issue refunds. However, my belief was met with a massive amount of positive energy. Only a handful of copies came back with that 200% return policy attached to it.

The message in the book was so compelling that even people who would have previously scammed the system by trying to get the 200% money back guarantee or simply took offers like this to make money didn't even try. Instead, people changed, participated, and validated the existence of Secret Entourage.

The lesson to be learned here isn't that you have to go all in or you cannot make it, but rather that you should strive to create innovative products that push the envelope of human behavior, not just products geared to make a buck. When you manifest your talent, you end up believing in the work and therefore going all in isn't much of a risk at all. It's simply reassurance and unbreakable belief.

The *Third Circle Theory* book and course became a hit. The demand for help increased significantly after people read the book. Once again, we expanded upward into yet another vertical revenue source. Each vertical involved recycling the resources or customers (which I will cover in detail in the next chapter). In this last attempt, I decided to leverage both the client base of *Third Circle Theory* and the existing resources in the form of video interviews of some of the most beautiful success stories heard to date. With more than 30 video interviews in our archives, we had a great resource for developing a series of written articles with beautiful imagery.

The $1,000,000 Directional Shift

In three weeks, we agreed to create an online platform that would leverage existing work to provide an upsell to our free model. We weren't merely creating content, but bringing to life the valuable knowledge resources we already had.

The Secret Entourage Academy was born; it was far from pretty, but it was functional. The goal was to secure one hundred featured interviews as fast as we could. With the power of social media, we quickly achieved that milestone. Our online self-education platform focused on bringing together accredited entrepreneurs to teach their specialty. Even though, at the beginning, it wasn't very clear or beautiful in its design, it quickly became evident that people who supported our brand and *Third Circle Theory* trusted in us enough to stick around while we figured out every single detail.

In 2013, the birth of the Secret Entourage Academy happened and in 2014 marked the rebirth with version 2.0. We built and launched a beautiful, interactive, and content-filled academy with a clear navigation path and the gateway to taking the Secret Entourage brand to 1.4 million dollars in revenue. I had surpassed the seven-figure plateau in a whole new industry again with a whole new team and the connector that would help link the rest of the brand with the baseline for building an empire.

The Consulting Parallel

Secret Entourage was growing. Those who were paying attention understood the power of branding and social media. They wanted that same growth for their brands, and so the calls started coming in, this time from much more affluent companies that wanted to break into the lifestyle or online space. From $100,000 yearly contracts to $25,000 website designs, our resources quickly became strained. We barely maintain our growth.

We made the decision that one company wouldn't be able to scale. It would be too limited in its growth in comparison to the growth of the other. What started as two sister companies ended up with two seven-figure businesses, one with a cap of five million dollars a year in revenue and the other a limitless company with a unique ability to open lots of doors.

Sometimes, you must stop and reflect on the long-standing plan and sacrifice short-term revenue for long-term growth. In this case, for the sake of the bigger picture. I had to accept my inability to scale my most profitable business, VIP Motoring, and the inability to continuously grow and manage Secret Consulting, a very lucrative business in itself.

"This was the by-product of choosing that money was a by-product of work, not just the alignment of opportunity" – Pejman Ghadimi

While I accepted that money-making opportunities were all around me, I also noted that I was actively creating them by doing the work. The more I worked, the more doors and opportunities opened themselves to make even more money. I realized that the shortage of money would never be an issue, even if I chose that the company's focus would have to be otherwise. I consciously decided that every single opportunity that came my way did not require me to act on it. If an opportunity was not directly aligned with the bigger picture I had in mind for my existing businesses or the direction I was taking, I would simply dismiss it in order to remain focused.

I assigned a CEO to run VIP Motoring and decided that it wasn't the right time to scale Secret Consulting. Subsequently, all my focus shifted from working offline to creating an online hub for what would become my greatest business and entrepreneurial creation to date.

The Entrepreneur Within

Being an entrepreneur requires the ability to see farther ahead, so much farther that it would be very hard for others to even understand or predict if any of your projections were accurate. Seeing ten to fifteen years ahead is needed, but creating shorter-term goals is necessary, as the marketplace shifts in ten years, industries come and go, and consumer behavior changes also. Too many changes mean that creating a ten-year plan often leads to three-year disappointments. Instead, building a ten-year vision, backed by one-year goals, guarantees you move forward and remain adaptive in your approach to bringing that vision to life, even if that means you need to make a few detours along the way. Seven years ago, my vision was to simply help educate and shape the future of self-education, but my yearly goals changed as the momentum I created by doing the work opened new opportunities. As I mentioned earlier, each one I brought to life sparked yet another three more possibilities. The idea then wasn't to decide which to take, but how to ensure I fostered the right talent to seize all three and any others that would come along.

My partners, Alan and Navid, did eventually become the individuals needed to sustain the work and effort needed for the growth of Secret Entourage. While the journey was filled with laughter, disappointments, and even anger, it was a one that only the three of us could have survived.

The secret to this partnership was like unlike any other partnerships. We were like a tripod, but we weren't fixated on which leg did what. Instead, we focused on maintaining the equilibrium, ensuring the balance would not be disturbed by our inabilities and personalities. It was as if this tripod supported a camera—which was Secret Entourage. The camera could only capture sharp images when it had sturdy support. Our shortcomings would create an uneven balance. Nevertheless, our ability to constantly extend ourselves to catch the other person's shortcoming meant that our common goal was not centered on <u>why</u> we weren't stable, but rather on <u>how</u> to stabilize the camera. What we needed to do wasn't about us, it was about Secret Entourage and the mission itself.

When you build a business with partners, you must find partners who believe in what you are doing more than what is in for them. The destination and importance of reaching the goal must be understood by all, as well as believed in until the very last minute, even if that comes with great personal sacrifice. You must believe that what you are working for and on is more important than your personal feelings about it. The belief is what holds the focus to the very end. While I acted as the constant glue in the relationship, I also made sure my partners' independent progress would lead to a place where they needed less and less of me as we grew to closing in on our vision. Our goal was to make sure each of us understood our responsibility and pushed ourselves to the next possible plateau.

The Perfect Spider Web: The Foundation of an Empire

Now that you understand the background of how the baseline of all my companies came about, I want you to see a very simplified diagram that shows you the two most important aspects of building an empire, and not just a business or brand. Maintain the constant pursuit of becoming a better recycler in your customers and resources. Once you understand the baseline, I will break down for you each component in a simpler manner that allows you to replicate this process in any industry.

The reason I shared my entire background with you is so that you can see how I have applied these same principles to my own businesses, hoping that you will understand how to re-shape and re-engineer your thinking to allow your product, business, or idea to scale. Scaling is the single most important aspect of business, as a stagnant business is dead long before it knows it.

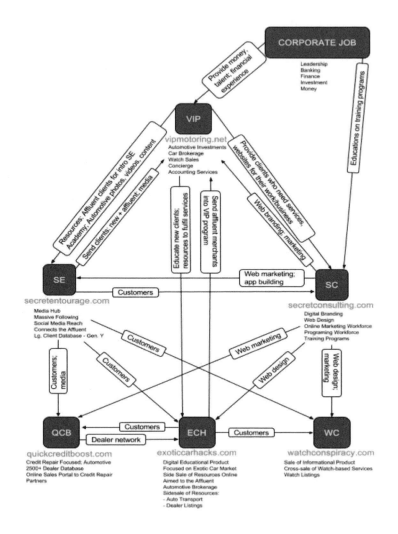

In this next section, I will walk you through the core business principles you need to understand to be able to take your business through the RADIUS cycle. I will simplify the concepts to enable you to see how and where your business fits into each. This approach should make it easier for you to identify what is missing or what needs to be enhanced so you can progress.

SECTION 2: Reaching Across Different Industries Uncovering Solutions

The RADIUS model encompasses the breakdown of people, product, business, brand, and empire, with each of these having its own pillars of support. There are many intricate details that go into each of these components; the model I will teach you is based on verticals from a new perspective. Long gone are the days when you, as the creator, had to put yourself in the shoes of your customers, to design products you wanted to use yourself or even focus on the idea that advertising on TV was the only opportunity of mass public reach. Today, the world has changed and the access to information, businesses, networks, and the interconnection of everything and everyone, has expanded the playing field significantly. People may believe that the marketplace is saturated by millions of new people who are opening new businesses, making it harder than ever to become relevant due to the mass competition, but that is simply untrue. Information allows access to more people to start up a business—and perhaps more startups do exist than ever before. However, the ratio of start-up to success has significantly decreased, with even fewer entrepreneurs succeeding today than ever before.

So, why does the market feel saturated?

We are now playing on a global scale with players who have always been playing, but who couldn't previously play with you, since barriers of reach existed locally. This is the same effect as video games consoles. It's not that more people are playing video games; it's that you now can play with people worldwide instead of being limited to people in your living room. This may seem intimidating, but it is actually an opportunity to understand that, while your competitors can reach in your area for clients without even physically being there, you, too, can reach into theirs. This provides for a new way to think of business—one that is global and requires quick and swift action.

The First Pillar: People

People are at the core of everything: the start, the end, and everything that happens in between. Regardless that you lead people, sell to them, influence them, or build a business with them, they are the lifeline of any business. Furthermore, any single person's success can usually be attributed to the people who helped along the way. Even if you consider yourself a one-man team, your ability to push past your own limitations holds as much weight as everything else described here. The way people integrate into the RADIUS model is quite simple and is broken down into three categories.

1. People come up with *ideas.*

2. Ideas *reach people,* and people are limited *in time,* which translates to the most important core principle and goal of this pillar being…

3. *Ideas reach people in time.*

1. It All Starts With An Idea…

Where Do Ideas Come From?

There are many types of ideas that formulate in people's minds. There are ideas where you see others act upon a variation of a concept you once had in mind. These ideas came to you, but came with no merit or ability to act on, are the real ideas that you not only get passionate about, but more importantly, take action on. Many people get the first and second types of ideas, but very few get the more relevant and crucial third types of ideas. The ultimate question remains: Why do some people find such great ideas all the time and take action, while others with the same great ideas sit back and do nothing? The answer is simpler than you think and comes back to the core fundamental that all ideas— even if they originate from you to begin with—are not always the right ideas as they pertain to <u>you</u>. Everyone can come up with ideas, but only people who align themselves to their ideas are able to turn them into action.

All ideas fall into two main categories: ideas that fill people's need and ideas that provide a solution to a problem.

<u>Ideas that fill people's needs:</u> Your customers have a need, and you have a solution. That solution doesn't have to be revolutionary; it could be as simple as identifying the lack of a nearby coffee shop. Establishing a coffee shop would help you fill that void for those people needing coffee in a certain area. Another example would be opening a store or showroom because you recognize the need for such a service or product where you live, which others haven't fulfilled. This approach leads to money faster as the processes are already established allowing you to follow through and basically put A, B, and C in place in order to get D (revenue or money) – It's really as simple as it sounds, but it isn't easy.

<u>Ideas the solve problems:</u> These are the ideas that solve a real problem that has yet to have been assigned a solution by anyone. These entrepreneurial ideas will require a lot of thinking, hard work, constant planning, and years of tenacity to bring to life; and it is possible that years go by before you even see a dime as a result. You must not only be prepared for it financially, but must have the tenacity to stick around long enough to be that person that brings the idea to life.

There is no path to success. There are only the behaviors that exist within you that can lead to achieving success. This can be a huge undertaking. The primary reason so many people fail is they take on this task without experience, or the understanding of themselves.

Both types of ideas described above have principles that can lead to a successful outcome; one requires a significantly greater amount of work than the other. This is why it is so important to differentiate and segment the ideas into the two categories. If you are indeed in the right position to bring the idea to life, you must align the idea with yourself. This step is simple is and requires only that you understand this basic graphic as it pertains to needs-based ideas only.

The diagram above represents the essence of how ideas are born; they are the combination of three key elements:

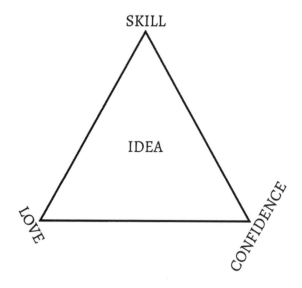

Love

Love matters, and it is the best place to begin to identify the topics that arouse your curiosity enough to follow through.

Love leads to curiosity as it pushes your interest to learn more without being forced. You can call it a voluntary curiosity. If you love cars, then you are never really working as you research and learn about them. It feels like fun, but you are constantly enhancing your knowledge of them without actually doing any work.

Confidence

You need confidence if you are going to be in business. You need confidence on the topic at hand, which is why you must focus on ideas that linger around topics you love, as it's easier to research when you are passionate. The more research and education, the more you understand the topics and can better identify the patterns to grow your confidence of the subject. When your confidence reaches a certain level, you tend to analyze and understand a few things better than others all together. This ability to enhance your confidence in a niche allows you to develop skills around that aspect of it. Look at it as the more you learn about automotive mechanics, the more confident you become in your understanding of how engines and cars work. Eventually, you can take that learning to action by confidently working on cars themselves.

Skills

This component is one that you can either have, learn, or delegate, but the required skill must be there. Following on the example above, you can learn how to work on a car, or run an auto shop. Either way, you have the ability to follow your passion with your accumulated confidence. You may choose to look at the series of skills needed and then decide those that will be learned and which must be delegated to partners or employees. It is the understanding of the model that either enforces the first two or reminds you that perhaps the idea you have isn't aligned to your current ability.

These three core elements must follow their course in this same order if you wish to see your idea come to life.

The Evolution of An Idea

When dealing with ideas that solve more serious problems, the three-point graphic takes a bit of a different evolution, as you can see below. Most of the problems that lack a solution in the world must be fixed through innovation, which is much more difficult than providing a simple service or product. It is about creating a sustainable solution, educating an audience on its existence faster than any other competitors in the marketplace, being able to spread the solution, and make sure the solution's adoption reaches the mass market. As you can imagine, undertakings of this size are much more difficult and require a heightened level of awareness, self-capacity, and emotional intelligence. The result is simply an evolution of our previous graphic.

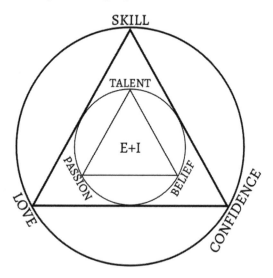

The three components evolved must be looked at as the same ones as in their enhanced mode.

Passion: is purely the evolution of love. While love is an emotional feeling you cannot always explain, passion is an evolution of love that combines it with action and creates a constant flow of action as it pertains to the subject or topic of your emotional infatuation

Belief: is the evolution of confidence. Your confidence comes as a result of believing in yourself, and belief becomes a projection of that confidence in something other than yourself. It is also your ability to forfeit your immediate needs for the greater purpose of something you hold more important than yourself.

Talent: is an evolution of skills. When skills are practiced and mastered, your natural abilities to exceed manifest itself. The enhanced ability or skill is once more the competitive advantage you hold over anyone else learning and competing against you. That manifested talent or enhanced skill is, therefore, the place you need to focus on, always staying ahead of others who will leverage their own skills to catch up to you. But it is in your ability to foster your inner talent that you will find the success you seek.

The lack of Talent, Belief or Passion is the key reason various people have small victories and countless failures before being able to experience one massive victory by eventually combining the three. When people start engaging in solidifying these three components found in the first triangle, and as a result start understanding the traits of the second triangle, then they gain enough momentum to not only undertake larger problems to fix but also have a higher success rate in doing so. This is mainly why I always recommend that people consider starting their journey into entrepreneurship by learning to enhance or simplify existing solutions, rather than attempting to innovate industries by creating new solutions. Several of today's biggest businesses like Facebook, Apple, or even Tesla may seem to be innovative in nature, but really started as an enhanced solution.

Furthermore, it was only through that success that the evolution of the innovator led to the improvement of the business simultaneously. Look at Facebook, for example, a business that didn't create social networking, per se, but improved it. Facebook was far from innovative in its launch, catering only to a few colleges and universities, and providing very limited enhancement over what existed such as the social network known as MySpace. Facebook's innovation took place through the CEO Mark Zuckerberg's adaptation, growth, and understanding of the real problem that needed to be solved. Facebook first addressed a need—connecting college students in an online social network—and evolved into solving a problem. Many businesses whose products you use on a day-to-day basis started with similar principles like the iPhone or the electric car.

The key takeaway here is that although innovation and changing the world may seem like a very attractive proposition, the journey to get there may need to start on a smaller basis. Allow yourself to evolve into the person who can support such an invention rather than being tested by your inability from the very first day. Everything in business and in life is linked to an evolutionary process. That process in entrepreneurship is your evolution as it pertains to your skills, confidence, and love.

2. Ideas are Only as Good as Their Audience: Understand Your Reach

While ideas and the types they fit into matters, the greatest asset in the power of such idea is understanding how big of a market it can reach; not necessarily in its existing form, but rather by the end of its evolution. Creating niche products and services is great, but is also very limiting and counter-productive to the idea of broad reach. I often recommend for people to consider their reach in the following manner before embarking and starting production on their idea.

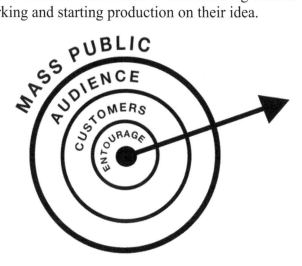

The goal in reaching an audience is not just to sell them a product; the idea of having an audience is a business in its own—as an audience is nothing more than a group of people connecting to you because of shared visions, ideas, or beliefs. When building an audience, you are ultimately creating what we call *reach*—the ability to influence people across a defined spectrum with a message. When people create businesses, their goal is to reach their customers, and in return, those customers purchase and support the business. It's a symbiotic relationship.

When entrepreneurs create businesses, their goal is to create an audience. Both might seem the same, because they are separated by a very fine line. Many in an audience are indeed customers, and many customers are part of an audience as well; however, these audience members are very different than typical customers and the contrast once again can go back to comparing entrepreneurship to business.

Creating an audience and creating a customer are different. Creating a customer is closed in nature and transactional, while creating an audience is open and relationship-driven. Both are profitable, but an audience can be leveraged more than once over time, while the other cannot. Businesses create customers, while brands create audiences. Businesses share their products, whereas brands share their ideas like Tesla, for example, which doesn't just produce a better electric car but has created an audience that believes in a better world with less pollution; but both ultimately start with people and hold a common goal of reaching more people.

Must We Understand Why People Follow Us?

This is a question often posed to leaders worldwide, and one that can be turned into the context of a business. It may seem to be a very generic question at first glance. The level of thinking required to answer it will shock you, as the response is not to be answered from your belief, but rather from the beliefs of those actually following you.

You can ask a group of ten people why they follow you, but will not identify a real and genuine pattern until you have a following of at least one thousand people. Why? The reasons people decide to follow varies so much that, in order for a true and effective pattern to manifest itself, one thousand people must be sampled to achieve a reasonable pattern. Then, you must assume that all the people who were tested will answer with honesty and not in a subjective manner.

Every follower can be broken down into three types, as there are three key reasons anyone follows.

Emotional Connection

The business or person creates an emotional connection for the followers, which shares a common belief very close to their hearts, based on their past experiences. If a business focuses on creating solutions for veterans in need, it would naturally attract those who experienced such pain and struggle. People who immediately related, based on past experiences and the emotions felt when they had no access to a business like yours or a person like you when they first needed it. There is a deep emotional connection, even if it is to the idea itself. Typically, this type of connection creates the strongest type of follower, as belief is blinding, and there is even an element of love involved. Many charities and organizations worldwide (even terrorist groups) recruit people to support their cause by primarily manipulating their messaging with the emotional connection, to create diehard followers whose deepest beliefs align to theirs, no matter how expressive such followers have previously been or not been.

Logical Believer

The practical followers are those who completely agree with what you are doing—for example, someone whose life was made easier as a result of you or your product's existence. They had a need you filled and problem you solved. The use of your business, or its product, is what these followers are after and often are more technical in nature as they first focus on the technical effectiveness of the product. They even often focus on providing constructive feedback, desiring to help you improve the product or service your business provides.

Intrigued Disbeliever

This category is by far the most interesting, as this is what we typically refer to as haters or people who are against our brand. In reality, they are confused followers who want your service, but are afraid to admit it works, because their past beliefs prevent them from accepting its concept. As a result of this internal struggle, they feel the need to be involved in discussions by sharing feedback without ever having tried the product or service. They have zero understanding. Their past experiences with similar situations dictates their tones towards you and your business. In due time, they turn into logical believers, as they see you are still around after some time. Should you fail, they will be the first to say, "I told you so." Should your business continue to grow, they will become great advocates. You will recognize them as those haters and disbelievers because they remain involved in conversations around you and your products, which believe it or not, still means that you are on their mind even if they do not want to admit it in their days of discovering you.

Once you break down the three core categories, limit your sample of one thousand followers to the local believers and intrigued disbelievers. They will better help you understand if you indeed are on to the right idea, and how the market will respond to it. The emotional connecters will automatically support you, no matter what. Finding your first one hundred loyal fans is very hard, but not as hard as finding your first one thousand non-loyal followers, which is certainly necessary.

From Sample to Audience to Customers

Believe it or not, we all have a sample of people following and supporting us— even if we have no product to sell. This is typically your entourage and it consists of your family, close friends, and acquaintances. Most of us cannot immediately think of one hundred people we call friends, but we certainly can come up with at least that many people we interacted with, known, or connected with on our day-to-day lives. This group of people, no matter how close or disconnected from you, has always been your immediate sample. They are the ones who, no matter what you do, will always be your immediate critic and, most likely, your best assets or worst enemies—depending on how you look at it. This is why it's important to surround yourself with incredible people, especially in daily interactions. The job of your immediate circle is to provide feedback, regardless if it is solicited or not. They will be your first line of defense to overcome and gain acceptance from in order to move forward mentally. Either they will provide great feedback with quality criticism or they will discourage you by telling you how useless it is.

The other function of this group is to become your greatest press asset to create your first line of reach. Meaning that it typically is within that group that your idea will start gaining traction because people will discuss your product or idea, share it with friends, and, if they like you, will even strategically position your business in front of useful contacts for you, especially if they want a piece of the company as well.

Nonetheless, that sample will be your first infiltration of creating an audience. This is normally why individuals with celebrity influences and friends leverage them early on, and, in some cases, don't even have to ask them to share the idea, as it comes naturally. You may also have noticed that certain PR agencies will send gifts to celebrities in hopes that they will wear, display, consume. or participate in sharing such a product. Indirectly, their goal is to leverage those celebrities' connections to help businesses build this very same sample. As you may imagine, this is also why starting your second, third, and fourth business is much easier as this group is further engineered with quality individuals from your first attempt.

Once the sample is penetrated, the reach to an audience becomes a natural progression and the marketing part comes into the picture. Finding friends of friends or targeting the same types of people with similar interest all comes into the picture (hence, Facebook is a multi-billion-dollar business). The goal of finding an audience is to understand clearly whom who to reach and how. Contrary to most people's beliefs that your audience is exactly the same as your customer base, the purpose of your audience is basically to listen to feedback, hear comments, and participate in making sure you are aligning your marketing to your future customers, similar to a focus group.

Once perfected, the model can now change to the attempt at gaining customers. This shift might be sparked by your audience, but will also significantly expand the audience as you blend the feedback into your business. Your perfected approach enables you to reach more people, ensuring your business has a voice. You can share how your business will serve those who trade money for the product or service you're offering.

Think of the goal of the audience as the referees to helping you understand your value proposition. Once you value proposition is ready and accepted by your audience, the next goal becomes to introduce your product or service to the crowds. This is usually the shifting point of when a venture becomes a business and start rethinking its process, instead of only focusing on its innovation or quality. There are some things you need to consider about the mass public as you increase your reach.

1. Your Audience and the Mass Public Are Very Different.

Think of an audience as being a warm lead, offering feedback, communicating, following, and engaging. The general public isn't warmed up to you, and therefore, is quite the opposite. In many cases, you will encounter negativity, poor feedback, and unconstructive responses from the masses. It's a knee-jerk reaction to something they don't know or understand—unlike your audience who has already interacted with you first and then your product. When people interact with just a product, they rank it solely on the basis of their experience with it, because they have no context of what led to the product. A very good example is my book, *Third Circle Theory*. While the book was very much eye-opening and life-changing to my audience with 99 percent of people loving it, the mass public at times ranked it poorly because of one simple typo within its pages. This type of negative market reaction seemed very isolated at first, but it is more common than you think and should be expected as part of the process, rather than as part of a problem.

2. Don't Expect Support. Expect Money.

The whole idea of going from an audience to the masses is to reach more people, which ends up bringing more awareness, and more importantly, more profit. Don't expect your audience to be supportive of your vision. You may still gain a loyal following in the masses, but there will be many people who buy your product and never use it. Others buy your product and don't see it as you intended. As discussed in *Third Circle Theory*, this is the reason why being emotionally disconnected from your product is the key to ensuring its growth. Don't take it personally and use the revenue generated as the measure of how well accepted the product is.

This is the first phase of turning an idea into a product, brand, and empire. You must understand that the farther you reach, the larger the impact, and the more powerful the acceptance. You can correlate each reach aspect to each growth phase.

Entourage – Idea

Customers – Product

Audience – Brand

Mass Public – Empire

In most cases, you can also correlate the revenue growth to the same level—even if this isn't true in all cases but still within the majority.

Entourage – Idea – Worth $0

Customers – Product – 6 figures

Audience – Brand – 7 to 9 figures

Mass Public – Empire – Billion and up

By understanding this correlation, you will be able to understand why your business is stuck. You can correlate your business's growth and failure to one of the attributes of each stage.

The stage of ideas is usually worth nothing as it starts with the validation of those you can immediately reach, your entourage, at no cost, to give you real-life feedback on the idea itself.

The stage of customers creates a price and structure of fulfillment by selling enough product. When companies sell a product, without thinking of branding, they are often met with new opposition with each new product and the need to re-engineer each new beginning, like Motorola having to convince you each time that their latest phone is a better option than competitors while Apple's minor tweaks to the iPhone make it a no-brainer to their customers. You will learn later how to overcome such issues in the long term.

Some business owners can launch new products without building any brand, but they typically do not break the seven-figure mark. They remain stay stuck in a six-figure yearly game. What I mean by this revenue is by taking the 10-year scope of revenue and dividing it into each year as an average of what the yearly revenue is. Many companies may launch a product and generate over a million dollars in revenue during year one and then lose money yearly until the product's demise. The average revenue across the lifespan will, in most cases, equal six figures annually if executed properly.

A Good Brand Meets a Good Customer.

The idea of branding comes from scaling the reach of multiple products or services, and creating a concept of consistency that allows an audience to form. based upon consistencies across the entire product line. For instance, Apple has mastered branding. Every electronic they sell is known for its simplicity, reliability, and design—three core traits that every Apple user has come to expect from them. Apple realizes their loyal followers maintain these expectations, so they do not stray too from it. Each new product doesn't replace a previous one, but allows Apple to reach other segments of the electronics industry. This is the way you leverage products to grow from audience to mass public. In the case of Apple, if each product is worth several million dollars in their early stages and eventually evolve to billions, then the combination of similar products targeting different people allows them to create an entry point for all segments of the mass public consistently recycling its audiences over and over. The compatibility of such products and enhancements of the experience with the combination of two or more products allows the handcuff model we discussed earlier to become a reality for its customers, meaning a customer remains dependent on a product—like hardware—from past software choices. This allows a customer to be more forgiving based on the need for the convenience of the other related products. If you don't like the new iPod, but have 5000 songs in your iTunes library, the integration of the iPod with iTunes will hold more relevance than the extra features of the new iPod.

The final stage of the mass public is farthest from the core of your idea's beginning. This is important to note from a visual standpoint, because it is also why it may shift and change so that the mass public will adapt to it. In this stage, you will see another reason why separating your emotions from the product is necessary. The variations in the product's functionality and design might be essential for an entire society to adopt it.

Reaching a mass audience is achieved more effectively when done in single businesses. You can attract different groups for different reasons into a common brand under different companies and for different reasons. There is not a universal product. There is a way to filter a niche—or to a specific audience, you may say—and then expand and grow into mass market. Let's take body soap as an example. Dove, the soap manufacturer, may be known for its higher quality soaps, body washes, and shampoos, but it's most talked-about products are not generic soaps, but specialty soaps for women. It is easier to provide higher-quality niche products and enable the reach to spread the farthest.

Let's analyze this.

Women's soap (specialty) – Core advertised product

In order to successfully add lines of soap products for men and children, they target women as their core audience, as they are the primary people who shop for and purchase soaps for the household. In some cases, this shopper is also the consumer, but shopper marketing experts recognize that there is a distinction between purchaser and end-user, so they adjust their marketing to influence each one.

While new products are introduced for new segments, the same customer base that is satisfied with the previous product is targeted to purchase and bring new Dove products in the household, rather than targeting an entirely different market segment. In other words, Dove understands that woman are most often the one who make the buying decisions of their products, even if they are not their end-user. This is called the "80-100 model" which I will share with you shortly as well.

This insight into a household's buying habits enables it to be branded, even though different people within the household whom in most cases may not even know have access to the same line of products and are habitual users of it. Also a core reason more soap and shampoo products are targeting male audiences is because they realize the void in the marketing of such products and identify an opportunity, like Old Spice, which points out being a man as their core messaging.

As I mentioned, the farther you reach, the farther you go from your core idea and its message. Your focus changes to meet what the market wants, which is why many diehard users of your product accuse a brand of selling out to money when the company seems like it's no longer paying attention to the original messaging or audience. The company is not selling out; it is enhancing its reach. The more revenue generated, the more people you can reach, and the more capacity to broaden that reach, which is why you must adjust to what works, rather than what is the best of the capacity of the company.

Take many of today's automotive manufacturers as a perfect example. Many car manufacturers are saving money by recycling parts rather than creating the very best possible products, as their goals are to balance out their ability to continuously reach more people—which includes building more affordable vehicles. They are not making the cars they want; instead, they are making the cars that sell. This is why one-off manufacturers of specialty cars are bringing such premiums to their cars. Even manufacturers like Lamborghini and Ferrari are in the business of selling cars, more than in the business of winning races. Twenty years ago, an automotive brand proved itself based on its racing history and amount of victories, but today, it does so, based on the numbers of units sold. Race technology can fuel the future of a brand, but it holds no relevance on the brand's perception of quality, craftsmanship or experience. This is why, when products reach certain masses, they are backed by so much more money, board members with specific business experience and more as the equilibrium of growth must exist rather than a simple vision.

3. Reach Has an Expiration Date, and So Do You.

The core of the RADIUS model is to understand concepts of business that will revolutionize your perspective on growth. One of those ideas is the "recycled concept" that allows you to scale multiple verticals simultaneously, without losing focus or growth from your core business model. Understanding this model requires you to understand these simple concepts first.

Every Business Operates on an Expiring Timeline

That's correct, every business and every entrepreneur has an expiration date. No matter what you work on, the customers you reach, or the industry you operate in, the time in which you exist and the resources available to you are ever-changing. The opportunity you once identified will eventually expire and as a result take a different shape. For instance, being successful in the nutritional supplement industry 15 years ago is very different than it is in now, based on various factors, such as social media, marketing, ingredients, regulations, etc. A plan that may have had a significant impact then may not even make a dent in your bank account today. The sooner you accept that every opportunity is like a door slowly closing, the faster you walk through it and realize that the only thing preventing it from closing is your ability to adapt to these changes, proactively pushing your expiration date farther.

As a result of understanding this basic concept, you are able to project a timeline, or should I say, "time-based lifeline", for your idea as it stands today. Another example that falls in this ideology are the Internet cafés, which were popular businesses ten years ago when computers and Internet access were expensive. Those owners should have predicted that technology and the advancement of it would mean that eventually everyone would have a computer. The same can be said with Blockbuster's inability to predict the rise of on-demand platforms like Netflix. This type of short-sightedness can—and did, in this case—lead to serious business disruption that could end a business and create a serious financial loss.

Ten-Year Vision is Only as Good as Its Yearly Goals.

People often confuse vision with goals, due to inexperience or the simple fact that they do not differentiate themselves from their ventures, businesses, or ideas. People regularly correlate their personal goals and rewards with their business vision—a huge mistake that is fueled by a society that promotes capitalism and a constant reward mechanism. My vision, for example, with Secret Entourage was to bridge the concept of self-education. To date, this venture is not related to any concepts of personal gain on any levels. Should the vision of Secret Entourage come to life, society will likely reward its acceptance with money, but my ambitions and monetary goals are not associated with my vision. They are only related to my abilities of creating a company for change that has an attractive long-term vision, backed by yearly goals that create sustainable revenue.

Creating a ten-year vision allows you to look far enough in that lifespan timeline so you can recognize if you are indeed working on a problem or business with enough pathway to last. We often overlook this concept and look at the rewards along the way, rather than at the outcome we wish to create. Any business whose life expectancy does not exceed ten years is not going to become a sustainable venture, and certainly will not become the core or foundation of an empire. Empires take time to build and short-term businesses are simply money-making opportunities, not really foundations worth building on. You must be able to see far ahead—to look past basic things like revenue—and understand if the word legacy (the idea that a business would exist past your personal existence) matters. If so, then the need will exist to find ways to create longevity by creating measures above and beyond money.

The One-Year Plan Times Ten

After the ten-year vision has been established, then comes the need to create a plan of direction. I only mention "direction" because once you go into battle, you maintain your objective but the path to achieving it may change immediately once the bullets start flying. A plan of direction does not dictate what actions will be required, as it is likely all are changed by the time you are faced with the execution of such actions. Take your ten-year vision and simply divide it into ten milestones that will bring that vision to life. Each breakthrough must represent a building block on which no previous one can be missed, as you are building a foundation while you are bringing a vision to life. Any milestone that could potentially be missed and still allow the business to move forward should not be described as a breakthrough. Imagine you are building a home, and that each milestone is a structural aspect of what actually holds the house together, rather than an aspect of decoration. For instance, foundation cement cannot be skipped, as the house would never withstand any storm. What flooring choices or paint you put on the walls cannot be used as structural and therefore cannot be used as milestones.

Once you establish what the ten breakthroughs are, then go back to the beginning. Define the core goals that need to be met to reach the first milestone you have. Keep in mind that without each breakthrough, the business cannot progress, and therefore any unmet goals steer the business towards its expiration. Yearly goals must be compounded into one outcome only by answering this very question: "Will meeting these goals reach our milestone?" If so, then you must do just that, as the livelihood of your business is at stake.

The reason the core focus is only a one-year goal to a milestone is because, as each milestone and the timeline of each milestone is met, the following milestone or year's worth of goals could change as a result. The direction may change, the execution pattern may change, and the following milestone may be tweaked, based on your compounding return of knowledge.

By reaching each milestone, you are fortifying the vision or allowing the vision to move in a different direction, which is why planting ten years of goals is completely useless. The learning, skills, confidence, and the discovery of everything related to it leads you to tweak and re-evaluate your original vision—a perspective that was based on your previous understanding of the situation. This is why politicians are considered liars who are incapable of sticking to their promises. Their understanding of their four- to eight-year term in office is based on their understanding of a situation which they have acquired as a result of a certain set of information, but upon entering office they are given real information that they previously had no access to - giving them now a new set of information that changes their understanding of how to achieve their goals which as a result change the plan all together. They underestimate the job altogether.

Progress is built upon foundational blocks of movement. No movement means no progress. Essentially, the main goal of any business is to move forward or in any direction rather than staying stagnant. This is also where the phrase "perfection kills progress" comes from, with perfectionists delivering their product or service too late, as they are met with a changed market platform that no longer has a need or is now filled with competitors ahead of the curve with real market data.

Understanding yourself, your reach, and your limitation in integration into the market enables you to validate whether your product is indeed on par with your long-term vision. Remember, successful entrepreneurs win because they look farther and connect the dots forward as much as they validate their effectiveness by also looking back.

The Second Pillar: Product

The second pillar of RADIUS is about understanding that products are brought to life by three concepts:

1. Connecting the dots forward;

2. Getting to the starting line; and

3. Becoming an efficient bridge builder.

1. Connecting the Dots Forward

We covered the difference in Pillar One of solving a need versus solving a problem; and looked at the importance of understanding the evolution of the person you are with your capacity expanding overtime, as you undertake heavier and larger problems. The main link here is to ensure that, even in the earlier days of facilitating needs, you are still aligning the simplified needs with the problems you want to solve in the future. Remember that the RADIUS model is about continuation and aligning your opportunity's lifeline with your very own lifeline, creating one continual evolution in which your personal expansion allows the expansion of your business. If your ideas all roam in different realms, you must be able to create a connection point somewhere along the way. For example, let's say you want to create cup holders that for a very niche car like the Tesla. You may also want to be an "automotive blogger or journalist", which is very broad. While these ideas may seem to be connected by the sole notion that you love cars, they are also connected in another very important form. One can be the transport vehicle to share or talk about the other. Finally, perhaps a third idea may be to have a tuning shop (which is once more aligned) by having now a place of expanding cup holders into more cross sells.

Let's break down this idea in a very simple manner so you can see this in action.

Niche idea/product: "Tesla cup holder"–Very limited in user base, very limited in reach. Expansion is possible as it piggybacks on a trend: electric cars (e.g. Tesla).

1. Automotive Blogger—Very large possible audience, low revenue (saturated) and piggyback on original product by blogging about a specific niche, reducing the reach as well as broadening the product reach. When you blog about Tesla, you reach a wider audience as there is interest in Tesla, even outside of its car owners. But the product can only reach people who own Teslas; therefore, you just expanded your customer base, plugged in your other product and secured your marketing while creating yet another form of revenue. Most blogs fail because they rely on old forms of ad revenue, but you will rely on sales of your own product.

2. Tuning Shop—You may want to start a shop to tune cars, but you will already have an audience of Tesla owners who want upgrades for their cars, so you can create more products to add more opportunity to your first idea, and give your second idea one more revenue opportunity, and content that leads to even more revenue. If the third idea costs too much to start as it's more capital intensive, then focus on the first idea until it can support the third idea. Focus on using the second idea to limit your spend and increase the capacity of the first idea, while getting you closer and more prepared for third idea. Eventually, you will have enough money, leverage, free marketing, and products to launch Idea Three and continue to fuel the engine that will have established your business with everything it needs to undertake a brand concept.

I need you to understand how to connect your ideas and leverage all of them by connecting and tweaking their approach to one another—rather than chose one, fail, give up, and restart.

"My entire empire was founded on the idea of connecting rather than shifting, which is why I never gave up on an idea. I knew even when it wasn't accepted that another idea farther down the road would help reshape the previous ones."

2. Negative One Hundred to the Starting Line

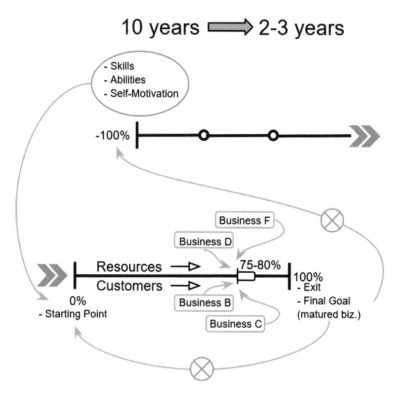

Many people make the typical mistake of assuming that, when they make a decision to start a business, they will start at zero and end when they reach their personal full percentage at one hundred. Reality is that starting a business often requires a foundation, and while many want to go straight into it and get to the hard work and profits, they often overlook the simple idea that, without foundation, you are working against the current. Think about it this way: You can either build a canoe and row your way against the current, or do what most people do, which is jumping in the water and swim. Regardless of the way you have to work, position yourself to be able to survive a longer journey. I know that the concept of jumping in first is very attractive, but the likelihood of success along the way diminishes greatly as each year goes by. There is a saying that goes, "Entrepreneurs jump off the cliff and build the parachute on the way down." The reality is, how can you build a parachute if you don't even know how one works. It's very possible you figure that out as you are falling to your death.

You are more likely to survive and succeed if you have a foundational idea of the direction you must take once you jump in. Understanding that, while action is the key to differentiating yourself as a success from a failure, researching and building a foundation is part of that action, even if it seems like you are standing in the exact same place where you started three months earlier.

The momentum may not be increasing, yet the ability to gain more momentum and move faster is what you are building. More importantly, ensure you focus on aspects of your life and business that are in your hands only, rather than allow external life factors to slow you down even in this entry phase.

Foundation is Built Off Three Key Pillars:

1. Work ethic

2. Knowledge

3. Self-awareness

No matter what industry you are in, what innovation you seek to create, or how much money you begin with, these three key concepts determine whether you are going to be faced with obstacles or simply your business's death.

Work ethic comes down to your ability to look at work from a different lens than society has provided you. The sense of balance—like a 40-hour work week or the freedom of time you believe business and entrepreneurship will provide you—are all preparation for failure, not growth. Remember that when you work for others, you have this benefit of structure, which has taken them decades to create within a working business model. When you work for yourself, you agree to give up such structure, which requires you to also give up the idea that your work hours can be structured equally. This goes far beyond the idea of showing up for a job, but rather understanding that there are no parachutes, no bailouts, no paychecks, and no guarantees—other than knowing your efforts are directly correlated to your results. Effort in itself is also a subjective word, as we all have different definitions of this, as we do of "work ethic". I have always used this explanation when trying to define "effort" and "hard work". If we accept the fact that more than ninety percent of small companies fail in their first twelve months and another fifty percent of that in the following two years, then we can conclude that being in business is hard; but can we really say that so many people with hopes and dreams are lazy? I would hope not. As a matter of fact, I am pretty sure that many of these people work longer hours, sacrifice much of their finances and family life for their business—and so comes the ultimate question: If a person with the willingness to put in the hours, eagerness to sacrifice family time, and is prepared to put himself/herself at financial risk everyday with the hope of winning, then why would you think that doing the same thing will guarantee you success? If they work hard for long hours, do their homework, show up, and still fail, then why would it be any different for you, just because you are willing to do the exact same things?

The simple answer is that it is not any different. Your work ethic is not about long hours or sweat equity, but rather your ability to work ahead of the curve and adapt, something many people miss. You see, most invest their most precious asset time by working in their business. This is done not only by making sure everything is working fine, but also by managing your day-to-day activities and focus on productivity. Profitable days are the core of what makes a business thrive, but the reality is that if you work in your business on a daily basis, no matter how hard you work, you are only as good as the direction the business takes on its own. When you only work hard, you are not steering your ship onward; you are merely rowing to stay afloat. The work ethic you need to have is your ability to work in your business as needed, and to devote extensive time working on your business, looking ahead on your off-time. Your daytime is needed to survive while your nighttime is needed to steer and change direction to ensure you are choosing and actively working on reaching your destination. The difference between those who understand this critical difference and those that don't often ends up in the simplest of form of success or failure. Work ethic is about working ahead, not just working.

Knowledge is another key factor that people often overlook—sometimes due to arrogance—as the idea of failure seems to scare people more than the desire for success. This, in itself, is a problem, too. I admit that I was very arrogant when I established Secret Entourage, assuming that many of my past successes would automatically translate to the future growth of a new industry at an accelerated pace. I was met with much resistance. As a result, I lost three years of growth to research that should have been done beforehand, and not as I moved ahead. Assuming a business will be disruptive to an industry without data is what I call arrogance, and I had fallen victim to it. Now, there is enough data, capacity to research, and leverage for anyone to self-educate prior to starting a venture. There is also enough information to make educated decisions rather than those based on sheer belief. Belief will keep you alive when things get tough; being knowledgeable will prevent you from heading in all the wrong directions, causing you to lose belief. Knowledge comes in two forms: the idea of research and the idea of testing—both of which are boring and will slow you down when you are eager to jump in and just crush it. Research—while you may assume to be enough by searching the Internet—isn't as simple as that. Research requires more than just using a search engine; it requires interfacing with people— through conversation, discussion and live interaction—who are in that industry.

The key to great research is a diversification of perspective. Look at the same problem through three distinct perspectives:

1. The consumer's

2. The owner's

3. The industry leader's

Three very distinct views of the same problem will uncover aspects of the business that you might never have considered. Once the research is in, then comes the ability to validate the idea by figuring out its leverage. Any idea can be a good idea with the right execution, but some are much harder to get off the ground than others; and while market validation doesn't tell the whole story, it does indicate the difficulty level. When we launched Secret Entourage, we knew that the market wouldn't accept the concept. We would need to work against the current; however, in the launch of Exotic Car Hacks (another business I started), the exact opposite occurred, as the market loved and accepted the concept— making not only its launch easier, but also helping to grow its revenue in six months to what Secret Entourage took six years to accomplish. Market validation doesn't dictate how successful something will be, but how difficult it will be to make a success. When validating, remember to measure two core components. The first one is how much the market wants it. Understand how many people are willing to pull out their wallets by doing a pre-order or a pre-sell for 90 to 120 days prior to launch. Worst-case scenario means you can issue refunds, should you not move forward.

The second one is the organic factor of its growth. Are all your efforts focused on paying money to gain attention, or are others discovering the page and sharing it. The more attention something gets, the more organic its growth. Even bad attention or criticism means people care enough to talk about it. Even good artists who are hated by the crowds are still selling plenty of albums. Measure the viral nature.

Self-awareness is the Essence of Being Grounded.

This is where most people who jump into business too early typically fail. This is the reason I recommend people solve smaller problems first. Work for others or discover how the workforce works, before attempting to solve the bigger problems out there that disrupt how industries operate. Being grounded means understanding that you are not special and that you comprehend the scope of where and how your project truly makes an impact. It's the understanding of the equation of life, rather than the need to redefine it without merit. If you think you can change the world, when you have yet to change your own life, you are what we call "delusional" in the business world. Too often, business plans come with billion-dollar evaluations and ideas without prior track record. Too often, people assume they are the next Elon Musk, Steve Jobs, or Bill Gates; yet they struggle to balance their own checkbook. This is the core of understanding the *Third Circle Theory,* which teaches the essence of disconnecting yourself from your idea and understanding that you are indeed insignificant until you prove you have created significant value for others. Aligning reality with direction enables a clearer route to fuel your belief and vision. While it can change along the way, the sense of direction must exist at all times or you will end up swimming in circles until you eventually sink.

3. Bridge the Cash or the Skill

I typically don't invest lot of money to start any business. It does not mean you must follow my choice. You may need as little as a thousand dollars to incorporate your business or build a prototype. One thousand dollars may not be much to many, but it can also seem like lot to some. We are going to look at how you can bridge the need for start-up funds. Your idea of world domination may be grand, but it can also be short-lived if you are not willing to get out of your comfort zone to see it come to life. You might have to sacrifice your existing fun or time to bridge your lack of funds. You need to become a good bridge-builder at this stage, as you must constantly build bridges to overcome your shortcomings, regardless of whether the reason is lack of money or skills.

Here are some ways you can look at bridging the gap in case you needed examples.

- **Sell things you don't use, or can live without:** Believe it or not, you may have to sell furniture, jewelry, watches, video games, books, musical instruments, car, etc. Sacrifice must start somewhere and, trust me, this won't be the biggest one you make.

- **Get a part-time job:** You may hate working at a drive-thru or bartending, but if you believe in your idea, then work additional hours when possible and save every penny you earn towards launching and building your new business.

- **Start a different business:** The idea you may have may be great, but it may also be too expensive to undertake as a first idea for someone with limited resources. If your goal is to sell exotic car clutches and each one will cost you $5,000, then perhaps you may want to initiate a different type of business that requires less capital in order to eventually raise enough money to move forward your original idea.

- **Leverage skills instead of capital:** You may be required to leverage some of the costs in exchange for skills. This may seem primitive, but it is best to keep moving forward even when you lack money, which means that, whenever possible, substitute things you typically pay for in favor of learning skills to get them done yourself. This won't be easy or comfortable, but perhaps necessary. You may need a website as a core need for your venture and may be forced to learn to code so as not to remain stagnant in your execution. Far from ideal, but a possible path to moving forward.

- **Get a partner:** Partnerships are never easy. You may lack skill or finances to start. Perhaps someone else who not only believes in your idea but shares different skills than yours can participate in building your business. Partnerships are usually the go-to strategies that most entrepreneurs look to, as being in business is a very lonely road to victory and many would rather not travel through that alone.

- **Raise capital:** Partners are great, but investors can also be great or evil. You may be forced to look at that as an option to getting the baseline you need to get started. It is a good way to raise start-up capital, if you can select the right person. This should really be your last resort, rather than your preferred option and we will explain why later on.

- **Crowd funding:** Got an idea that people would kill for? Then prove it and raise capital for your start-up costs and prototypes by crowd funding. The power of crowd funding isn't simply the capital you raise, but also the market validation you obtain. You ultimately gauge the market's acceptance of your idea and its willingness to pay for it.

- **Defer the expenses:** Registering a real company or building a perfect prototype can come after you have acquired some sales. You can always pre-sell a product or service. You can even allow some sales to occur before perfecting your plan.

- **Get creative in the marketing:** Facebook ads may be the way to sell your idea, but may cost money. Instagram is free (and perhaps a dozen other platforms where you can reach people without hard costs). So, you can leverage one platform to pay for the other by pre-selling or selling a product.

The world of business may or may not require money, but these few examples demonstrate various ways you can ensure money doesn't become the reason you start or stall. Instead money becomes the leverage you need to grow. The most important part here is that you will have to give up your comfort to facilitate what you lack on a daily basis. This may even require you to give up time with your loved ones or buying your kids presents on their birthdays. The beginning may be filled with sacrifices, difficulties, loss, heartbreaks, and pain. It is the reason why many would-be entrepreneurs don't get very far and blame their failures on lack of capital. It is their inability to sacrifice the "now" for the "later" that halts them and pushes them back to their safety zone where they remain stuck. Regardless of whether you need a $1,000 or $1,000,000, you will need to understand that money is never the reason for failure. It is your inability to adapt to how to make money that will lead you to failing. You must learn to bridge your comfort zone above all from comfortable to uncomfortable.

These three core principles now take you to the third phase of business—a phase that has most people failing in their first three years. Partly because they do not understand the "People" and "Product" phase in an attempt to consolidate everything into an easy solution in order to make money. Money, while holding a very important aspect in the world of business, is also the biggest misleading indicator of reward. Most equate success with money; however, money should be associated with process.

$ fun PROCESS!

The Third Pillar: Business

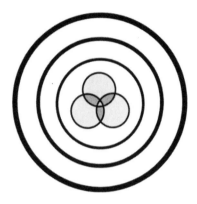

Business is about money. It is the vehicle that enables reach. The vehicle for reaching others to embark on the change is business. Even in the cases of entrepreneurship, the end goal is to facilitate change. This is the reason there is such a fine line between business and entrepreneurship that often creates massive confusion across the board when people start with either one. As you can see from the graphic above, the main fuel for a business is money.

The reason why most businesses fail at making money and ultimately close their doors, is because they focus solely on that—making money. Wealth is made by people; it is the by-product of others transferring their money to us. During the old days, when money didn't exist, people were only as good as what they could produce in exchange for what they wanted to purchase. People's worth was based on what they possessed and created to trade with others for the things they wanted. It was always about the exchange of value.

As people grew without skill or value, they traded their time to help others create those very same values that people wanted. As a result, they were given money for their time, which, in return, they could trade for more items of value to them.

When you enter the world of business without understanding how money functions in an economy, you are met with an enormous opposition that will eventually drain your capital. This lack of knowledge is due to only being able to understand how to trade your time for money, and eventually diminishing your own value and depleting what others will pay for your time, which will be putting yourself out of business.

To succeed in business, you must understand three core concepts as they pertain to the RADIUS model: the law of supply and demand, the rule of 0 - 80, and the creation of a customer.

1. The Law of Supply and Demand within the RADIUS Model

Understanding basic economics means having a clear picture of what impacts price, value, and cost of product in a business. It also means uncovering unique opportunities, based on unfulfilled needs. There are many factors to a global economy, many of which revolve around currencies and public affairs. There is one universal aspect, regardless of the country you live in or the business you operate. That is the *law of supply and demand* and it reaches far beyond just understanding its correlation on price.

The basic premise of this law underscores how the factors of demand and supply impact someone's willingness to make a purchase. Higher demand for a product and less supply means that the seller can charge a higher price. For example, look at the higher price of special edition versions of your favorite products. In addition, the limited release of newer items making their entry into the market are priced at a premium such as gaming consoles by Sony and Microsoft, which always cost 200 to 300% more in their early release months, but go much lower as time goes by. In the same token, the opposite is also true. Less demand with greater supply reduces the price of the item as there are too many units. The more supply exists and the more the true non-inflated value of the product shows itself (meaning much closer to its cost of making it).

Law of Supply and Demand as It Pertains to Marketing

If a business can find the sweet spot where it meets just enough supply to force its demanding customers to make a purchasing decision at the moment, it does not need to lower its cost of goods sold (COGS), as the value is perceived based on the lack of immediate supply. For example, an ad promotes an offer that is limited to the first hundred people, forcing the focus on immediate action with the implication of limited supply. The idea to limit the supply can be found through three components:

Limited Time: The supply will run out in X days or X hours.

Limited Edition: The supply will always be available, but this version of it will not.

Limited Entry: Supply isn't limited, but access to the supply is limited.

Increased demand, coupled with limited supply, means the amount of product sold is likely to increase and continue to do so until it is completely sold out. You must understand this essential marketing concept so you identify it, and be able to duplicate it, as necessary. Comprehending how consumers make buying decisions enables you to tailor offers that are relevant to them, and drive sales, not just views.

Law of Supply as It Pertains to Financial Markets

Financial markets hold significant relevance on the law of supply and demand—in part, because the markets control the buying power, and in the United States also controls the credit system. Financial markets are very predictable, since they are influenced by the most important resource in business: money. When people lose money in the markets, their spending behavior changes itself by spending less. When they are making more money, their spending dollars go up.

Due to the vast number of investors playing at all levels, a simplified pattern can be found easily even if it doesn't apply to all. This is very black-and-white for the luxury market, as you analyze investor behavior in buying luxury goods when markets soar and their willingness to dispose of luxury goods when markets fail them. The common public, on the other hand, plays into the same role differently as financial markets impact their day-to-day lives differently. Their cost of living fluctuates—based on the costs of housing, gasoline, food, and healthcare. Therefore, this segment controls the demand for products more so than any other groups. When the common public, who typically has 500 dollars of disposable income per month, now has 1,000 dollars, they gain more buying power. As a result, more people are willing to buy more to begin with. Thus, they control the demand more than the supply as they are the primary consumers.

Both of these components come into play more often than you think. During the 2008 recession that occurred in the United Sates, many people lost significant amounts of money on the decline of the housing market; meanwhile, others lost money on paper while holding out for a stock market recovery that would never come, not even to date. Let's understand why the law of supply and demand plays its part here.

In 2005, there was a shortage of houses and an increase in demand, due to banking institutions giving easier access to credit. This flood of buyers caused home prices to rise at a faster pace than usual. Beyond a certain point, prices were inflated high above the real market's actual value. The common homebuyer was willing to pay above the home's true worth was in order to obtain it, based on speculation that the market would keep going up due to increased demands. To a certain degree, this is healthy as it pushes pricing of goods that may be undervalued to reach their peak value faster, but it comes at a cost when the market can no longer justify the price of a good as it is highly above it projected value. In other words, everything comes to a place where it meets not only its perceived value, but also its ceiling—the point at which it is no longer affordable. The demand starts to go down.

When there is a financial crash like in 2008, the system will eventually balance itself out and return to an equilibrium. For instance, you bought a house that worth was $600,000 dollars but you paid $900,000, based on lower supply and higher demand. Then, when the market crashed, your home's value dropped to $450,000 dollars, due to the lower demand and higher supply. The actual worth of the home has been forced to become compliant to this very this supply and demand law.

The financial markets reset themselves on an ongoing basis, but that said, since the value hasn't changed, the home is now undervalued. This scenario creates a good opportunity to buy and hold, as it's going to go back up, even if it won't go as high to the original price you may have paid. At no point will the value do that as the crash will force the home down to

$450,000 dollars and slowly adjust it back up to $600,000 dollar (the real worth), not its inflated value ($900,000) as the bubble has popped. The reason the $600,000 homes sell for $900,000 will have forever disappeared, because it was never real to begin with. By the time the recovery rebounds the value to the $600,000 mark, the playing field would have changed. There were more houses on the market as the supply was still ongoing while the recession was happening, even if slower. The dynamics of the market that originally created such bubble no longer exists, because access to credit isn't as easy.

Understanding market adjustments allows you to anticipate consumer behavior ahead of the curve, not after. If you were a credit repair company or debt consolidation company—or had access to one—you could predict that, upon the bubble bursting, certain services would be in strong demand. Due to the high amount of customers entering the market, and the lack of agencies to fill those services, it would create an opportunity to capitalize on this new high demand/low supply curve.

Law of Supply and Demand as It Pertains to Skill and Labor

The same job today pays the same person 1.7 times more than it did ten years ago. Yet, the cost of living has risen over six times in most cases, just like fuel, food, insurance, and other necessities. But why?

Most people blame this phenomenon on declining economics along with poorly managed labor forces. The reality is, it is nothing more than a supply and demand equation when simplified. The skill may be worth 1.7 times more than it was ten years ago, but it is not rising at the same pace as the economy. The cost of the skill by itself only has so much worth. So, there is a finite value for the skill, and there is an influx in the amount of people practicing that same skill (profession). That means that ten years ago, there may have been one hundred coders to build a website in the United States, but today there are over 40,000 coders. Although a coder is only worth X amount of money per hour, that cost is diluted even more on the basis that the supply (labor pool) has increased significantly more than the demand (available jobs). Hence, the competitive nature means that the consumer (in this case, the coder's employer) has more choices and in return can drive the price down across the board.

The same theory can be applied to just about any business, which is why niche-based businesses typically do better than broad ones and can charge more for their specialized products and services. It is called the expert level, and allows a supply that seems to be much higher than before come across smaller as the specific duties become highlighted instead, showing a core focus and limiting the supply once more. There may be a pool of coders available, but very few are certified in specific code or have expertise so high that the pool of experts now is a smaller sub-pool.

If there are over 40,000 coders and all can do the same thing on the surface, then the value is dictated strictly by the demand at that time. But if you now say that only ten out of the 40,000 coders specialize in HTML 5, you are bringing back the value of the coder as the demand for the specialist is now greater than the supply. Creating expert-like niches in evolving economies allows the consumer to buy expertise, not skill; thus, creating a balance in favor of the individual selling that expertise rather than offer a skill.

Law of Supply and Demand as It Pertains to Forecasting Trends

This law can also act as forecasting tool to understand consumer behavior. By purely predicting what demands will be upcoming in excess allows you to identify a need for increased supplies. That means you can jump in and seize the opportunity to fulfill this upcoming demand. You can see this day-in and day-out in different hustles from people in respective industries, such as new gaming consoles coming out and selling for twice the price because others didn't re-order them and are now hungry for one. This also happens daily in the auto industry with new exotic cars that come out and are in short supply, but high demand.

Regardless of your industry, you can either predict trends and help facilitate the supply chain or identify alternatives as result of it. If you see a trend of smoothie bars coming up in your area, you can explore the increased demand and come up with alternatives products, or even look for a better way to do a smoothie bar. This can be very cumbersome and annoying if you're jumping into various, unrelated industries, but can be very lucrative if you identify the supply and demand elements ahead of time in your industries where you already hold resources and leverage. Imagine if you own a line of supplement stores and can forecast the "healthy eating" movement. As a result, you identify those products on your existing shelves that are made with organic or preferred ingredients to appeal to that crowd of people. You can, at that point, position to sell more by correctly displaying the product so it gets more exposure. You can identify upcoming products now so you are ready for the demand once it becomes main stream, or even go into a whole new vertical by making your own line of products that will meet that demand at the point when it is going to spill over into the mass market. This ability to forecast allows your vision to corner opportunities as you are creating them, based on mainstream trends, as opposed to being the last one to jump on and capitalize on them.

Law of Supply and Demand as It Pertains to Talent

The same concept can also hold true when dealing with talent in your organization. You look ahead and understand how consumer demand will require a higher level of talent in advance of the actual need. Consequently, companies that spend a great amount of time reactively hiring instead of proactively recruiting end up being six to twelve months behind their demand curve. They typically miss their opportunity to scale their business faster. For example, a large retail company that does not predict their biggest sale day of the year and is not fully staffed to help facilitate the sale's goal will fail to capitalize on the sales potential. The goal is to always use this formula to look ahead, evaluate all sides of the opportunity at hand, and then proactively position your business to not lose any opportunities that come with it. You can understand the correlation of upcoming talent with any upcoming higher demand curves.

Understanding how to manipulate the law of supply and demand as it pertains to your specific business will allow you the opportunity to capitalize faster and in a greater manner than your competitors. If you are in a business that is high supply and low demand, you must reconfigure your ability to present a lower supply while creating higher demand allowing you to take more revenue per client in the door.

2. The Rule of Zero to 80

The road to the starting line may have seemed like a drag, the road to the finish line couldn't seem any farther especially if your goal is to build a brand rather than just a product based business. You can look at a lightning-fast, Zero-to-100 business model if your intention is to build a product by forming a company around it. Those who do that can still make money, but often find themselves short-changed in the residual impact of business. I often coach such individuals to go back to the drawing board and rethink their agenda and direction. The idea of building a real business, even if it starts out as a product, is to create residual value for yourself. What good is the idea of working for yourself if you are constantly in need of working to accomplish the same results over and over again? If every day is spent with hours traded for income, then what was the purpose of going into your very own business to begin with? A person could argue that the point of being your own boss is the freedom of time, but the reality is that the freedom of time doesn't come from whether or not you work for others, but rather from freeing yourself from the dependency on money. You make enough money to buy yourself all the time you want, not the other way around.

If, from the very beginning, you do not understand this important, yet simple concept, the odds are that you will focus on building a company founded on the principle of just making money. There is a need for any company to grow revenue, but there is also a need for a company to establish itself and create a foundation for its longevity. This allows companies and brands to survive bad economic climates and ensure the brand name survives, despite ups and downs of business.

So, What IS the Zero-to-80 Model?

In short, it is baseline that a business needs to build to become a brand—from the starting line to a profitable revenue model, and a foundation strong enough to scale from. Most rush to scale a business. The RADIUS model, however, differs in that a slower, more controlled approach allows you to scale ten verticals, rather than one at a time. If you think of a conventional business model, then the point becomes to succeed in one business; and later start another and so on. Doing that is no different than trading time for money, and while with each exit you accumulate more capital, your leverage doesn't increase significantly. Think of the Apple model we discussed earlier. What if Apple had made the Macintosh and successfully sold it without ever creating new products or verticals, and instead started new companies to do it? This would mean that each and every time Apple would have been required to rebuild a fan base with the launch of a new company. They would have to start from zero to earn their trust, thus losing massive time between each product in order to become a household name. The other obstacle faced would be that, with every beginning, Apple would fail to secure a competitive edge over others as new competitors and the playing field would always be changing.

This may seem like a common-sense component. It also isn't always perceived in a black-and-white setting, like Apple. The Apple model seems common because most think of Apple as a computer company that sells many different types of electronics, such as phones, tablets, and computers. But Apple is so much more than that. The Apple model I am talking about isn't the multiple product concept that is visible, but rather the concept of computing—app distribution, streaming TV and audio, and much more. Verticals of growth are not just multi-line products. They are the results of two very distinct, recycling concepts, recycling your customers and your resources.

There are two types of distinct recycling concepts that the most solid businesses thrive off, in order to build their brand. They are customers and resources. Let's define the two before moving forward.

Customer: Not just someone who pays for your service, but anyone who is part of your audience and has shown interest by connecting to your business in a more serious manner than simply sitting on the sidelines. You can look at this as someone who has subscribed to your email list, bought a product, or follows you on your social channels. These people are your client base, have engaged in getting to know your products/brand, and share ideals that you both believed in.

Resources: Structural concepts you have created that support or grow your business. A resource can encompass anything in your more serious infrastructure, such as stores, technology, employee base, skills, talent marketing, revenue, and everything in between.

When building a brand, one of these two concepts must be recycled or reused with each new vertical you launch. If verticals can be built by recycling both customers and resources, then the perfect combination can be found and the verticals can grow faster and easier than ever before. If you launch a solid product or service, then you have a loyal fan base. If you launch a second product that is relevant to your audience, then you are now no longer paying to acquire a customer for your baseline, and so your vertical funds its own growth to the top—meaning that, in your original product, you had to find and acquire customers to grow the business, but with your second vertical, you can tap into existing customers who already trust you and are willing to take a chance, based on your bran integrity. You may have spent thousands in marketing and sold your customer one product and recouped that original amount, but now that you sell them this second product, you gain 100% of the profits when it comes to the acquisition. The goal is to understand that free customers are a powerful way to jump-start a business, especially if your baseline for customers is very large. Companies like Apple have customer bases so large that every one of their products can not only disrupt a market, but they can launch products that change market behavior as so many people are willing to invest only because of the brand name.

Looking at the same concept, recycling your resources means you can leverage technologies, workers, and more to build a second vertical without paying them more than you would have previously—allowing you to increase revenue with a new vertical without incurring the cost of a new team, learning time, or any aspect of support. For instance, if you are already paying for a team of employees to work on a project, then you can add to their responsibilities without increasing their pay. This may push them harder, but it will also make your investment into their salary worth it as they double up support, production, and more while working on a new revenue-generating activity. The idea is that if your existing resources can support more than one vertical, then their pay is split in half technically while your revenue doubles. This now makes your workforce much more efficient as well. This notion to look at resources as a scalable concept—one that looks five to ten years ahead. Ask yourself, "Who do I need to provide the support I seek—both then, and between now and then?" Then determine how to recycle such resources so that you can scale. For instance, in my previous example of what this model looked like for me, my ability to cross-pollinate staff and talent across multiple companies cut my labor costs, while improving the loyalty and dedication of each employee, as each was given an opportunity to grow significantly with each new company.

The Zero-to-80 model focuses on knowing where you need to head moving forward and actually making these two core concepts a priority, even if that means losing revenue or not making it as far. Understanding the importance of owning your customers and building your resources means you will spend your focus doing just that, rather than simply converting customers into revenue. This approach helps to create the core of a solid foundation, otherwise known as an infrastructure.

3: Owning Your Customer

Earlier, I explained that ideas have an entourage and businesses have customers, and people exchange money for the value you serve. But it is important to understand that customers evolve into an audience—a cluster of people who are interested in what you have to say or sell—when there is enough of them. The importance of scaling a business is to look ahead. Know that your audience tomorrow grows from a series of your customers today with commonalities, so you must understand more than just where to find a customer but whom you wish to serve.

Brands are the by-products of process, trust, and consistency (which we will cover in the next pillar). These three attributes bring you to a word that is extremely important to owning your customer and your business's future as it transitions to becoming a brand. The word I am referring to is "authenticity"— being true to who you are, rather than creating an image you think your customers want to see, it's the by-product of why people follow you and become your customers. We learned earlier that people are creatures of habit, and tend to follow one another based on reliability as well as a projection of their own love, fear, or desires. All of that converts into one word: authenticity.

People become customers because of your authenticity, which is often established in the business phase and then projected in the branding one. Authenticity is a combination of branding attributes and a projection of yourself into the business, which is why your reach becomes one with the business itself. If you are an aggressive person, you typically lead an aggressive business and vice versa. Nonetheless, this is important to discuss, as business owners tend to mistake how they acquire customers by focusing on why they believe people should buy their products or services; as opposed to being authentic and allowing people to discover who and what their brands are really about. In other words, you push out an image, hoping others like it and buy in, instead of projecting your real image and allowing those who agree to join you. This is no different than chasing money by constantly asking for it, versus focusing on the value you create and allowing others to trade you their money for it.

The way you must look at customers is no different than how we discussed looking at the business itself—as a timeline. Your customer needs to evolve with your business verticals, meaning that while you introduce new verticals of revenue and growth, they must also be advanced and positioned to recapture the same customer.

Here is a bigger breakdown of how we accomplished this with Secret Entourage. We conditioned our customers to online education presented in an appealing manner, giving us a competitive edge over our competitors. We understood that, by training our customers on the power of luxury lifestyle and on how to succeed in business, many of them would indeed move forward and pursue their dreams. As a result, Secret Consulting, a separate company focused on IT creation and marketing, was created to cater to their needs. I also looked ten years ahead, recognizing that as people grew up with Secret Entourage and found higher levels of success, that trust (branding) would translate to their need for luxury lifestyle. When they reached that point, I would offer them even more education, but this time on topics of interest like a platform to flip cars (Exotic Car Hacks) and watches (Watch Conspiracy). I conditioned them to be skilled, educated them, then helped them succeed, and finally educated them again on their reward structure. Nonetheless, it doesn't end there, as great empires are not founded on ending customer models, but recycling one to flow through existing resources. When the education part is done, I transition them back to becoming customers of VIP Motoring. This lifeline is a cyclical model that enables the customer cycle to remain a lifetime process, rather than a limited one. It is the ability to look ten years ahead that allows you to model the future consumer behavior and create verticals ahead of schedule, ready to capture the clients as you transition your business into a brand.

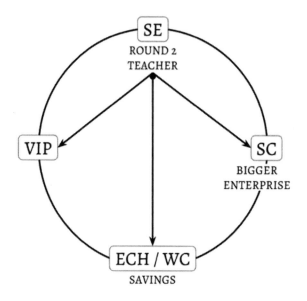

You may look at this graphic and wonder why the loop would ever keep going when there is no further need past VIP Motoring to repeat the process. Once more, you are about to find out why vertically integrated models allow brands to become empires in the next two sections.

The Fourth Pillar: Brand

"It takes one year to bring an idea to life, three years of survival to be considered a business, and ten years to be recognized as a brand." – Pejman Ghadimi

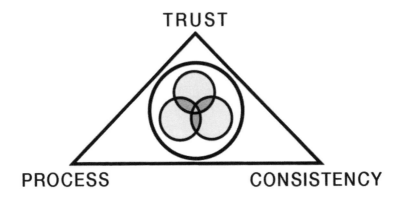

Branding is not about your words, but rather an intricate understanding of your customer's behavior and your ability to position yourself in a manner that is representative of what you want the next ten years to look like. You must ask yourself, if your customers are saying three things about you in ten years, what would those three things be? Then, work backwards to make sure the consistency becomes the reason that trust forms between your business and your clients. I remind most entrepreneurs and business owners that any ventures whose strengths are only an extension of their own behaviors and abilities will likely never become a brand. A brand is established when a business's vital attributes become its character and take its own shape.

How Brands Are Born

Opposite to what most business owners think, branding has very little to do with graphics, color schemes, and how beautiful something is. While those things do matter in the realm of being consistent in your brand approach or delivery, they are not the core of what establishes a brand. If we refer to the graphic above, three fundamental concepts must be present and consistent in order for the consumer to actually gravitate towards your company and accept those aspects that will be part of the brand's value. Your customers decide what your brand is known for, but it is you who sets the mood and strives to meet your very own expectations of what you wish to be known for.

Apple is known for three brand attributes: simplicity (why they still only have one home button on iPhones and tablets), design (which is why only three colors are available and every lines looks like one another), and reliability (which is why 90% of the updates done to your computer encompass a security update). These are the three things Apple did well in its earlier phases and that, over time, consumers related as powerful attributes of the company that became primarily its brand promise today.

As a business owner, you must earn the trust of your clients, because it pertains to those same attributes that matter to you. Be consistent in your delivery and make the process seamless so it can be repeated again. I will teach you how to look at these three concepts in a relevant manner.

Start with Process

Most people want to transition to new ventures in the first three years of their business, yet always remain stuck on the idea of compensating with being in two places at the same time. This mistake comes down to not having a process in place. Process is what creates direction for employees, customers, and much more. The more process-driven you are, the more efficient you become as you no longer need to do everything fast, and instead focus on improving each step along a well thought-out process. Everything from marketing to the physical delivery of your product needs to have a process, even if it involves a person navigating that process along the way. Your strategy to acquire new clients should be broken down into various processes, as well as your customer service issues. Without processes, there can be no delegation, no coaching, and no improvement, as every situation becomes a one-off situation that isn't repeatable. You become reliant on employees who may learn and know everything, but will put you back to square one the moment they leave to find employment elsewhere, because there is no sustainable process in place.

The key is to quickly adapt a procedure and use the first three years to perfect it to the best of your ability. This allows you, your employees, and your customers, to get used to the way you do business. The more efficient your business becomes, the more capable you become as a CEO. Process is not always in the way you do things as it pertains to chain management. It can also be highly focused on your core business values. One of the major processes for my company, Secret Entourage, was the idea that our website had to be image-centric and exciting in its delivery of information. Our goal may have been to become another incredible blog, but our delivery was always to appeal and differentiate through beautiful photography and the lack of advertisement on our pages. This process in delivery of information remained true since day one and only improved in its delivery with more striking photos, better placement, and a more appealing, overall design. While the process of design evolved for our business, that core value that we chose early on to make a process is still very much there today. Another example is our escalation of the service process for VIP Motoring. When we started, we were small. We gave our cell number to every client to make them feel special, supported by a promise to answer any concerns at any given time, 24/7. As the process improved and we grew to over one hundred monthly clients, the commitment and quality of service to our clients didn't falter. The exact process remains in place for the customers, but on the internal side of business, it is now managed efficiently by adding a layer of customer support to filter which requests require an account manager and which can be answered and handled directly by our service team, composed of eight service employees. So, the client still calls the same number they dialed ten years ago, but after hours, we added one more filter before connecting to a real concierge. This helps us scale the process, while having created a support system to ensure the same level of personalization, despite the increased amount of support needed to manage the larger customer base. By maximizing these systems, as a CEO, I was able to step back and train another CEO to hold down this vertical while I focused on building another business of revenue. It is easier to train people on how to maintain systems and improve them based on feedback, rather than having them start everything from scratch and figure it out without your vision in place.

Be Consistent in Your Delivery

Once the process is established, you need to get people used to that very same routine. This is the place where your leadership skills come to play. Consistency is a broad word as everyone has their own expectations of what being "consistent" means. People who are new in business often expect one year of their constant behavior to bring many rewards, but reality is that most businesses must exercise three to five years of consistency to start seeing the residual effects of their efforts. When we first started Secret Entourage, I had a proven track record of success in business, but it seemed to have no bearing on the fact that our audience and potential partners still didn't take us seriously as we hadn't established ourselves in this particular space long enough. I recall that many people used to make empty promises, pretending to be interested in helping, only to disappear overnight. Then, after three years, they came running back, attracted to be in business with me once they saw the success. I used to get offended that the support was lacking, but I came to the realization that a majority websites go out of business in the first year. This was the reason many believed that, while my work ethic was strong, my ability to scale a whole new, unrelated vertical wasn't going to be present. What they failed to see was how interrelated all platforms would one day be. I firmly believe that you don't need support to get results; you need results to get support.

This methodology that others cannot share in your vision leads to the necessity that it is within your process that they will get an idea of your values, what you stand for, and how you will operate your business. People cannot identify with what's in your mind, but can understand and see your actions. This is typically why your progress in business attracts the interest of people who want to join you, regardless of whether it's as a customer or employee. It is your consistency in your actions that will validate their belief in your direction and build their loyalty to your business and eventually even link certain attributes to it. Today, many people know that Secret Entourage does not advertise anything or anyone we don't fully believe in, no matter how lucrative the relationship could be for the brand. Our VIP Motoring clients know that we are always about creating transparent relationships and they have come to expect nothing less. These consistent brand elements create the ultimate ingredient that turns a business into a brand: trust.

Allow Your Authenticity to Create Trust

When you become consistent in your delivery, you are showing people a side of your authenticity, and they confidently buy into the process, to the point that those consistent attributes become an expectation. Think about the checkout online. Almost everyone expects fast checkout and fast delivery, but not everyone accomplishes that. Amazon steered everyone in the expectation that one-click checkout and two-day delivery should be the industry standard; while it's not promised by all online retailers, this ease and speed is a common expectation, even if it's never been discussed. Amazon's branding is so strong that it pushes an entire industry to keep up—without go out of business. When your customers have an expectation that gets met time and time again, these deliverables become the brand attributes they relate to your business and they form the baseline for what your brand is about. People expect Apple to be reliable and virus-free; as along as Apple products continue to function well without crashing, then consumers will continue to buy Apple products, since reliability is their key-buying factor. If people have come to expect incredible designs from Lamborghini, then every Lamborghini car must impress the world with its design and engineering. The point is that when people trust your brand attributes, they are more likely to forgive your mistakes and will not reconsider their loyalty as a result of one or two mistakes. When people consume a product and have no loyalty to its brand, they typically immediately love or hate the product, making no effort to connect with the brand itself. If you order a cheap, third-party hard drive for your computer and hate it, then you would simply discard it or attempt to return it. Now, if you buy an Apple hard drive for more money and it doesn't work as expected, then your first reaction would be to try to rectify the situation rather than to get rid of the drive all together.

You believe in the brand enough that you are willing to invest time to maintain your trust in it.

Trust creates leverage for a business. That leverage is what allows a customer to become handcuffed without even realizing it to your business. The connection is voluntary and as long as it remains so, then you have created a brand that customers will continue to consume and become dependent on. Let's go back to Apple as an example, which I like to use because this brand is commonly understood by the general public. Apple, as discussed earlier, has key brand attributes, which are simplicity, design, and reliability. These three attributes can be found in every, single Apple product, but it is the trust that pushes people to continuously buy more products. These key branding attributes are external, but internally within the company, Apple is also known for its inter-connectivity from device to device, meaning they make the experience better when each device works in conjunction with another. This is the Apple "handcuff" model. First, you love the product and trust it. Then, you trust in its compatibility with other Apple products that guarantee the same attributes. This is a perfect example of how a brand becomes vertically integrated within itself to create hundreds of revenue models, all following the same branding model. The first step is to create the process, then make it consistent to earn the trust, and finally, to recycle it.

The Recycled Vertical Startups (80-to-100)

We spoke in the business section of the pillars about the 0-to-80 model. Part of that model is to create a process strong enough that it can be leveraged and recycled as support for more verticals and businesses. The point of this strategy is to build as effective as a process you can so you grow to 80% of your business life and can branch off (refer to earlier graphic in the 2nd pillar section).

Before we continue to explain how to recycle, let's talk about what business verticals really are. There is a lot of confusion surrounding how to define a new vertical as they are often confused with new products sold to the same client base.

A new vertical is much more than a product; it is the ability to use your resources or client base for a whole new business. This new vertical also allows you to either save money on resources by one of two ways:

1. Starting up with an existing team doing more work without pay; or

2. Taking a base of your existing customers and immediately having a baseline of users to support the growth of the new business.

The first 1,000 clients are always the hardest to acquire, unless you have a model in which each launch automatically gives you 1,000 clients, based on a larger client base that you already have in another vertical. When we launched VIP Motoring, we offered automotive-based services. We then ventured into selling timepieces, which made sense from a new product standpoint, not an integration of vertical because timepieces only recycle customers, not resources. New verticals require both resources and customers to get recycled.

On the other hand, when we launched enterprise-level accounting services and IT management services, we already had our client list and knew exactly which of them would be interested in supporting this service. In this new vertical, we leveraged the audience in order to generate a baseline, meaning in our first year, we managed to generate $200,000 in profit from those same customers on a whole new business venture, which prevented me from having to shell out my own money or leverage investor capital. Instead, I funded it with a business that reached 80% maturity and then generated the first 50% of a brand new vertical in 90 days. Following this model, you can scale many new businesses without having to repeat the work or cost of client acquisition. It is all made possible because of that one word we discussed earlier in this section: "trust".

When your clients trust in your services, they are willing to take a chance on you. They often already understand your process and consistency, making it easy for them to take a chance. Even if your expertise in this new vertical isn't as established as your last, your clients will relate the level of trust to their past experience—not the possibilities of failure ahead.

The same ability to leverage clients can be made by leveraging resources. For SecretEntourage.com, we built a team of marketers and coders. We were then able to launch brand new, unrelated platforms on completely different topics, using the same back-end team, which lowered the cost of launch. The less we spend up front, the faster we reach that level of 50% sustainability, making it easy to work on scaling, rather than growing. The same processes and the same abilities transfer quickly to new verticals with no learning curves and no additional costs. Some of the greatest new verticals can be accessed by simply understanding your team's strengths and methods, and simply re-assigning them to new projects, based on their past track records.

The New Starting Line

Think of this process described above as traveling on a ship on a quest to conquer and find new land. The main ship may be efficient and move forward quickly, but it can only go in one place at a certain time. You may have processes in place that allow your ship to operate with or without you. So, nothing prevents you from seeing your best workers or crew members and having them lead vessels of their own with smaller teams in the hopes of discovering more areas simultaneously. Your core ship may slow down twenty percent, but your ability to reach four to five locations simultaneously pushes your true victory forward to five hundred percent.

The point is to train, leverage, and grow your resources until almost everyone on board is in a universal capacity. Imagine you had 20 stellar superstar employees on board, and all you had to do is rearrange their seats on the ship in order to move the common interest of the crew forward faster. You would be able to hold down your slowest assets while your best ones would lead on and keep driving forward. The key is to foster talent and resources that can be used universally and then change the dynamics of their position. In one of my verticals, one employee is head of social media, but is being groomed to be CEO of another vertical that highly relies on social media to grow. In another company, my partner is great at coordinating everything and acting as COO; but in the new vertical, he will assume the role of CEO as his skills are directly more aligned to the topic of company B rather than A. Both these people will start with access to endless resources of past companies and have some time to adapt to their new roles, while having support until they are eventually ready to build their very own team, and eventually detach from the mother ship itself.

The idea is that, in the case of an exit from one business—or the collapse of another—the other verticals would already be well on their way to their own 80% optimum state, at which point they are becoming their very own mother ship. This ability to constantly integrate new verticals from 0-to-50% by using a previous business's 80% leverage allows the growth of your empire to look somewhat like this.

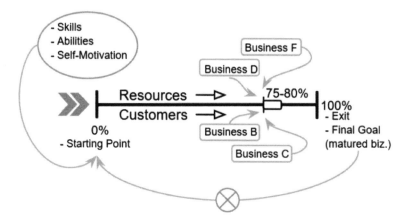

Map out the possibilities and be prepared to seize the opportunities you create, looking ten years ahead. Each new vertical must be identical in feel and process management, giving your customers a sense of belonging to the same family of businesses. Your designs must be consistent, your behavior, service models, etc., must all be aligned to the same core values. These values will not only carry through to your empire, but will become the foundation of your growth or fall.

The Fifth Pillar: Empire

Businesses that typically embrace branding understand that they are building the foundation for an empire. An empire requires your ability to keep scaling multiple verticals without exiting one or the other, thus triggering the snowball effects of residual power to carry on for decades, if not generations. Most empires are founded on the essence of one core business that is then expanded into hundreds of verticals. This can become so cumbersome that your ability to integrate into new verticals must be seamless and meet both the recycled customer and the recycled resources with each new vertical because, as many of you know, in business, time is never on your side. If you do not do that, then your ability to keep adding brands to your portfolio and growing them diminishes with each one, as time is scarce and no matter how effective you become, there are only 24 hours in a day.

Recycled Customers + Recycled Resources = Perfect New Verticals

Empires are built around the idea that perfect verticals are those that utilize both complete user (client) bases and resources as a means to launch. From the case of VIP Motoring, we integrated its user base into Secret Consulting, as only one integration was possible. In the case of Secret Consulting integrating into Secret Entourage, only resources were possible to be recycled, not clients. On the other hand, the integration of new verticals—such as Exotic Car Hacks and Watch Conspiracy—flawless encompassed both resources and user bases. This allowed Exotic Car Hacks to surpass Secret Entourage and its growth in less than six months from its launch. You may need to integrate one or the other recycling methods until you start seeing the vision forward enough. At this point, you can understand junctures where the maps cross at different points. Even if an integration of a company isn't possible today, it may be worthwhile to start the company and let it sit as automated as you can until you can come back to it.

This can be seen with my credit repair business. At first, this venture may seem disconnected from all other brands, but in the long term, it will integrate into financial education and much more, which will flourish into upcoming segments of other existing platforms, like Secret Entourage. Since the baseline of the business was established, grown and almost left aside as reactive. The integration isn't yet to a place where the business can be streamlined but when it is, it will be ready and simply become a plug-and-play business with a very low need for further scaling. The idea is to understand where and when businesses related to your team or users will cross paths, and determine what must happen for the capitalization of such crossings to take place quickly and efficiently.

Brands Consist of Carefully Created Exits; Empires Consist of Integrations

It is important to understand that empires are founded on the principles of building blocks, regardless of whether you created them or purchased new integrations. You can build multiple brands that could live off each other or purchase the missing pieces to ultimately create one giant pyramid. You can engage in an Apple-like situation and understand why buying "Beats by Dr. Dre", the headphone company, was a complement to many of their existing endeavors. The acquisition made sense, even though on the surface it may seem like a parallel of hardware that is very much not aligned with any specific business function. By understanding the longevity of the Apple vision, one can clearly see why a music hardware parallel opens many opportunities, including a partnership with a connector, Dr. Dre, who can help bridge the gap between Silicon Valley (Apple) and entertainment. With the pyramid, the pieces usually have to fit on top of one another, but in this case, they can be placed in any single segment in an attempt to complete the pyramid faster.

The idea is to link the effort rather than exit from it. One of the biggest misunderstandings is that pyramids revolve around a people, when in reality, pyramids revolve around a vision. I myself wish to change the way people learn and to improve the education system as a whole. My pyramid will have many components that are more obviously connected to this concept but the reality remains that if any of the foundational pillars of my business were removed, the ability to continue its growth with velocity would cease to exist. I highly recommend that if your goal is to build your own pyramid, you start looking at all your brands and businesses as pieces of the puzzle, rather than as leverage to move forward. While certain exits may be beneficial and aligned to the long-term goals, the concept is to connect the efforts and trust of the previous brands to build on a faster scale than ever before, not just to monetize. The concept of money must become a blur and the by-product of the efficiency of the processes in place, as any brand whose focus still remains as generating revenue is bound by its limitations as a business.

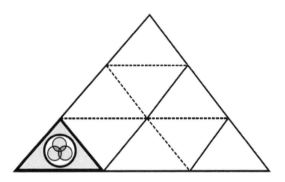

Vision = Position

Many of the business giants today, like Disney, were founded on the principle of vision, not money. You have to clearly define your position on your vision early enough. Understand that either your role is to leverage business to impact yourself or create change. This direction ultimately leads back to the core concept of *Third Circle Theory,* which revolves around defining if your goal is to start a business or be an entrepreneur. Both are ok, but empires are often built on the fundamental belief that true change can occur, even if it takes quite a bit of time to go from belief into reality.

The Ability to See Further

Most visionaries earn their titles because of their ability to see farther. As a result, they navigate a clear road map of what change they wish to create. Many who can only see as far as their own future typically are met with their own limitations or lack of understanding of current business principles. A well-integrated brand can easily enter new industries and verticals, gaining quick momentum with its buy-in and audience. For instance, Marvel Comics may have seemed as though it was limited to simply having comics and cartoons. When the right 3D visual effects met the opportunity to transition into films, in less than five years,

Marvel Comics became one of the most profitable and successful movie studios in history. This "takeover" happened as the right customers and resources were recycled and leveraged in due time. This is where the saying "opportunity meets hard work" comes from, implying that there is a time continuum. Your ability to position your brand for integration in various industries is what differentiates your ability to win when the right opportunity presents itself. I described earlier that I became involved in more businesses that had no integration at that moment when I chose to buy them. I knew that while they may not be relevant at the time, they would be, perhaps two steps farther down the road.

There needs to be a long-term strategy to the overall visualization of the pyramid. That can be done by reverse engineering the placement of each brand. There is a basic misconception that the first business must be the foundational unit that supports the pyramid. In reality, the first business could start at the very top and be the most insignificant when it comes to supporting the rest of the brands.

Consumer Behavior Meets Your Vision

There is the need to see farther in your business, but there is also the need to see farther in the evolution of your customers and resources. One of the best examples I can give you is how social media platforms go from a simple app to a massive household name. They have been able to integrate into each other by creating massive empires, as Facebook has done. Think about a social platform and how many people wish they could build the next Instagram, Twitter, or Facebook. Yet, not a single one of the people who have approached me as an investor with their social media idea get why the other ones worked. So, their pitch was flawed because they were not looking far enough into the future. They were assessing why someone should be on their platform today, which was irrelevant, as it would take them years to reach the mass market. At that point, even in the greatest levels of growth, these platforms would still fall behind, being too late to the party. So, how are social platforms created? And why is it relevant to cultivate not just what the future for your business holds, but also what is likely to happen to your customer base?

The rise of social media and its mass-market acceptance was more of a hardware play—combined with a shift on consumer behavior—rather than a software one. The rise of Facebook occurred when the smartphone outsold the old cellphone; Twitter exploded when texting was used more than calling; Instagram became the app to use when every phone became equipped with nice cameras; and Snapchat became what it was because video now dominates photos and every phone is equipped with an HD camera.

The companies that understood early on spent years adapting a user experience that would ensure that, when the mass market adopts a new behavior, it would be ready to provide the best experience. This is a very important example to help you shift your thinking in three dimensions, not in a linear way. When your resources and customer base are recycled, you have new verticals. As your ability to integrate more verticals grows to become established as an accepted brand, it is your ability to align your vision to the future of your industry that prevents you from crashing. This foresight keeps you innovative and ahead of your time. This is the key to working on your business and not in it.

As a founder, your job is to be working on the direction of your business. This role comes at the expense of examining and understanding what roads people are taking in their own lives and comprehending how your brands can interact and provide value to your customers today, as well as where they will be tomorrow.

I knew years ago that the Tony Robbins for this generation would no longer be one individual. Instead, he would represent the movement of people seeking mentors with similar values or lifestyles as them to get further in life. Because I projected, I positioned the Secret Entourage Academy to the future generation's need and their buying choices would be very different than what they were then. I also understood that people's views of the formal education system would change and fewer people would find it valuable to pay $20,000 (or more) a year to attend school. Creating a platform that took five years to perfect came with the understanding that it would be positioned best to take advantage of such behavioral changes and anticipate the future user base's needs.

Now that you understand that the stages of growth are for something as simple as an idea, it's time to recognize that business is a vehicle for reach, and not a vehicle focused on your survival. The faster you realize this, the sooner you start working on the principles that help you create real self-sustaining entities that have a genuine chance of becoming household names—and eventually, empires that carry your legacy forward. Too often, people start businesses with ideas whose sole purpose is to substitute their miserable income. As a result, they only create businesses that ultimately allow them to buy themselves a job, but never progress.

SECTION 3: Connecting Visions to Tangible Business

The Progressive Circle

In my first book, *Third Circle Theory*, I covered the essentials of the three circles that foster opportunity to discover your purpose and awaken the visionary within each of us. The three circles represent the following:

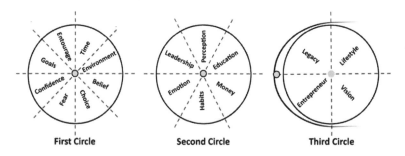

Circle One highlights the master of circumstance and one's ability to no longer remain a by-product of their environment, but rather a shaper of it. The pieces in the first circle signify different masteries needed to be in such control.

Circle Two reflects the mastery of society and the simple understanding that, regardless of our desire to belong to the same system and concepts, most of us want to break free. Still, we need to understand how to successfully play and learn within society itself, and then come to a place where we can eventually manipulate the environment by shaping it once more to our own need.

The key here is to understand that money plays a very large role in the leverage a person has on his surroundings. Furthermore, money can be a very effective tool to create progress for ourselves and those around us. We must learn to make it in order to shape our environment and define our role within it.

Circle Three represents the evolution of the mind and the mastery of living. Living rich is very different from living fulfilled. Holding onto high capacity and purpose is the greatest achievement one can reach.

The goal of purpose isn't spiritual, but rather one that eliminates the boundaries and possibilities of the first and second circles, which are mechanisms, create this very same sense of purpose and keep people aligned and productive but more importantly focused on one specific goal. This is good for those who need direction, but those of us who dream of a better life—one where we can make an impact on society and others—must live in a world where such boundaries are non-existent. Think of the first two circles as everything you are forced to do before your 18th birthday. The third circle is the start of your adulthood where you are held accountable to your own actions and given a chance to make your own decisions. The better you are in the first two circles, the more likely you will be in a good position to discover the third.

The key here is the conscious decision we make as to what we want our legacy to define about ourselves and the impact we want to have on others. This freedom of choice is always earned, never given, as even people who are born into massive amounts of wealth often never grasp their true purpose because they struggle to identify and differentiate their own mission with that of those who left them such fortune. Their lack of progression is often what prevents their ability to understand the effectiveness of the process. If you by pass the money element of Circle Two and go straight to Circle Three, then you are missing the experiences that come with it.

The theory requires the progression of the mind and the progression through key elements of all three circles. Finding your purpose and establishing your legacy isn't always built around the core of creating business empires. One could say that Gandhi and Mother Theresa both lived in their very own third circles fulfilled, even though neither held high positions of wealth and power through the lens of a business. Both were visionaries, but neither had businesses as the driver of their vision. *RADIUS* is about connecting vision to business, and to progressively scale such a vision while enhancing your character and capacity. If we account for all the different sections of each circle as described above then we can take out ten specific slices that constitute the key areas of focus that are specifically related to business:

The Progressive Circle is about evolution, as it pertains to experience. This circle is called "progressive" because business is about adaptability as much as it is about growth. Looking ahead is what helps to shape the direction and drive the constant growth.

The ten pieces that make up the progressive circle consist of the following:

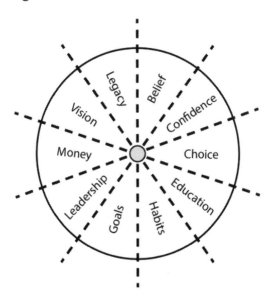

Each of these ten terms was found in the original Third Circle Theory diagram, but this time is viewed from the connection of the visionary, which in this case is you, to the future empire that you will build. Since it is progressive in nature, you must understand that the path through each phase isn't as linear; but rather an infinite loop of revisiting each step as a building block.

Each segment can be linked to each core pillar of a business. Each of these elements becomes the driving block of the transition. In other words, the ability to transition from one pillar to the next, such as product to business, is driven by the mastery of these specific concepts at each stage.

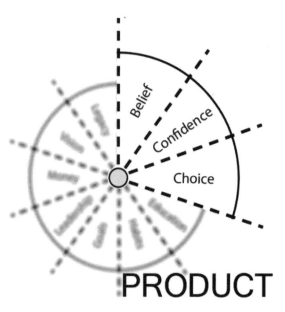

Stage 1

Belief is the starting ground on which products come to life, and the idea that a vision is a possibility. It's the awakening of the mind, and its acceptance that something that is unseen can become a reality seen by others. The belief is a by-product of other visions that have come to life in your environment. Such belief is then fueled by the confidence in the capacity to also bring such a vision to life. That confidence, as we discussed earlier, is the understanding of your skills, talents, and limitations coming together and now faced with a conscious choice that the only way forward is to actually bring the vision to life. The big point here is that the choice is conscious and voluntary, not based on the environment rather than the combination of belief in one-self, the product, and in the ability to bring the product to life. In the simplest of words, a vision is seen, conceptualized by the belief in its possibility, reinforced by the confidence of the possible outcome, and finally accepted as the choice for a valid path forward. This vision also becomes the internal source of motivation needed to succeed.

Belief Comes from Observation

Third Circle Theory explains that the formation of belief is heavily based on the observations you make of your environment. When you are exposed to negativity your whole life, you take on a "can't do" attitude. Someone who is brought up in a positive environment builds a "can do" future. When you surround yourself with incredibly talented people, you tend to notice their passion and the incredible possibilities of their vision. When you surround yourself with individuals who do not push themselves out of their comfort zone, you see people who always choose the easy path, rather than the one that will take them farther.

Let's look at this simple example. You are surrounded by individuals who are constantly focused on comfort rather than growth. You have an idea that requires you to build a prototype, such as a rubber phone case. Their feedback will sound something like this:

"Do you know how hard this will be? Do you know how saturated that industry is? What do you know about rubber?"

These are valid points, but they are driven on the idea of failure pushing your belief further back in rather than allowing it to bloom. On the other hand, that same question posed to a successful entrepreneur or people whose boundaries are not set by society will sounds different:

"Have you looked into the price of each unit? Have you found a location to make them? Who have you talked to that can sell them?"

These responses encourage educating yourself, using forward motion rather than resistance. This particular difference allows you to either suppress or foster this inner belief. Your response will suppress or foster your confidence in the idea.

Confidence is the By-product of Failure

The confidence to move forward often comes from your ability to differentiate between internal and external factors that can boost or burst your confidence. Confidence can be reinforced by the compounding effects of victory as well as its foundation is forged in your failures.

Failures will happen no matter what, and the best way to overcome them is to expect that any fiasco is not an end, but rather the opportunity to start again, empowered with the knowledge you gained from the experience. The faster you accept this, the less time you lose in between mistakes and the faster you reach a level where you can count your victories. Think of riding a bicycle. The fastest way to get to a place where you can race others is to start riding, learn to fall and get back up, and lower the amount of time that elapses between your falls. You will eventually race against others. The only focus will be to improve your time, no longer making sure you don't fall.

Push your confidence to also focus on growth, not on survival. Evolve your mind from "I can do that, too" all the way to "I can help change this." Allow confidence to foster in your capacity, not just ability. In this way, your choices can be focused on long-term success, rather than short-term gains.

Choose wisely, as there is no right or wrong.

In *Third Circle Theory*, I introduced the concept that there is no right or wrong in life, only in the choices we make. We often attribute a value to choices based on the outcomes, but we must also realize that each choice is a direction, rather than an outcome. Choosing to start a business is, in itself, nothing more than a choice; the actions we take dictate the outcome. Every action and every interaction we create after each choice we make in this phase creates a possible direction. The trajectory from the starting to the finish line is never a straight line. Regardless of how we define our choices, we need to ensure they are indeed taking us in the correct direction. You can constantly analyze your life and conclude whether the choices made in the past were driven in the correct direction, even if a goal was eventually met. The goal isn't to make constant choices but rather effective choices that relieve the need to make a six-year journey into one that will last ten years. Our goal as individuals is to find direction and align choices to enable us to navigate the direction to be met with the least resistance. Obstacles will arise on all grounds. We must learn to make decisions that help us flow with the current, allowing us more focus on the destination and not on those obstacles in our way.

Stage 2

For a product to become a sustainable business requires constant education—by the owner, for the team, and everyone in between. Educate yourself on the industry, its parameters, your competitors, and so much more. This education becomes the ground on which the necessary habits needed are established. The routines and the activities will create the processes required—which will lead to setting and reaching goals that take the business to that next phase.

Education Isn't Reactive

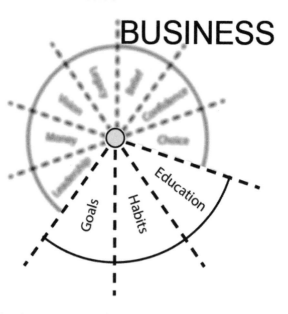

A big mistake people make in this stage is relying on partial and selective education, which means that they learn only to apply immediately such as learning to trade stocks only so you can make money, rather than just be more knowledgeable. More people only focus on learning technical skills they need to learn rather than understanding new perspectives. The flaw in the entrepreneur's mind is the constant need to fix a problem. Not knowing something becomes a problem in itself. When you don't know how to do something, you look for ways to resolve the issue. The best way to leverage knowledge and education is with enhanced perspective—the ability to learn new concepts and perspectives not always relevant to an immediate problem. You follow your curiosity to understand how things work, and you use education to progress and adapt. Recognizing new things enables you to enhance your perspective, which drives innovation and change. In many cases, concepts that leverage cross-industry strategies are the most progressive and innovative ideas, even though none are really the essence of new, but rather someone's ability to identify a trait or strategy and then pursue their curiosity.

Habits Come From Practice and Repetition

Good habits in this stage build from the repetition of the practices that work. The more you practice what you learn, the more you develop good habits that effectively deliver results, and the more consistent you become in the process. In this stage, you realize how much your actions can impact your business, both positively and negatively. The faster you develop good habits—such as structured business days, marketing practices and financial management—the faster you transition from a business focused on survival to one driven for growth.

Goals Focus on Growth

When goals are established in the earlier stages of a business, a big mistake people make is to hone in on "What's in it for me?", such as, "If I make X revenue, I take Y salary." So, all the goals become structured around your personal needs to get the business to a stage where your comfort is reached.

Personal satisfaction is important, but for a business to have a strong and possible future, you must be able to separate it from you. Force yourself to look at goals from a scale much larger than yourself. Examine the scale of the work, rather than the personal reward.

Money or revenue is leverage in business and is certainly a great measure of growth, but the growth of a business can be attributed to much more than its revenue. There needs to be actual growth that results from sales, product improvement, large contracts, reach, acquisition costs, and so much more. If your goals are to ensure you always have enough food on the table, then that is exactly what you are going to have—a business that manages only to food on the table. Every so often, you will be reminded that your direct effort will lead to keeping food on the table, and will have forsaken your chances to have food put itself on the table without your direct effort. Focus on the business growth, not its impact on your comfort.

Stage 3

With goals and structure comes the need to establish a team and lead them to a place that allows you to work on the business, not in it. The core idea of expanding becomes a possibility as the ability to leverage teammates to create amplified results becomes a reality.

The biggest leverage comes from the processes built in Stage 2 that allows you to have money that is useable for growth, rather than survival or payroll. The leverage of real money then comes in Stage 3, when businesses have enough to survive and grow. It is in the brand stage when the processes lead to excess revenue. A business that survives a month at a time cannot be considered a brand.

Your businesses become independent when you set up the structure to become a brand on the basis of a successful

166   www.SecretEntourage.com

product and excess revenue. You wouldn't attempt to turn a failed restaurant into a franchise, which is the same as saying you wouldn't make a failed product into brand or collective set of products. In Stage 3, you make the most important decision, revalidating the original vision. The difference between Stage 1 and Stage 3 is that, in Stage 1, vision is driven by environmental perspective, while in Stage 3, it is fueled by data and your clear understanding of what you are doing by an existing set of customers. In other words, one is a possibility, and the other is the by-product of the validation.

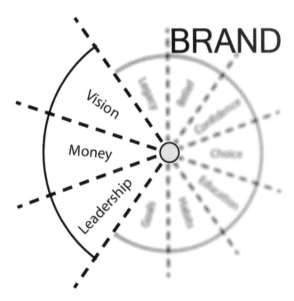

Effective Leadership

In Stage 3, the concept of leadership addresses a need more than a desire. Your ability must be made free of the people you surround yourself with. You must own the decisions and outcomes that come with them. Owners who never graduate this phase look at it as the leverage they need to gain freedom from working. They aren't paying attention to other aspects of business. This flaw leads to their escape from work, rather than their upward push. After all, the biggest perceived attraction to being a business owner in the earlier stages is the reward of not having to be at work while the business makes money. Therefore, now lies the importance of choice we discussed in stage two and the need to choose whether you move forward to become a brand or simply remain an effective and profitable small business instead. This choice must occur here, as it will significantly change the investment you make in others and the leadership style you choose to adopt in your business. If you choose the path of growth, then you invest in employees, their growth, and building a team that evolves with you. On the other hand, if you choose to focus solely on the revenue and your ability to satisfy your immediate needs, then your investment is only in the employees' immediate ability to retain and continue to support what you have built to date.

The leadership style changes, based on the goal, even if you are considered a good leader. Effective leadership in the realm of moving forward is about one core aspect: forecasting. You must forecast your human capital needs today, next week, and next year, and understand how to foster talent to meet tomorrow's needs with the people you are choosing today. The big difference is that it becomes an investment in people, not simply the decision of whom to hire.

As with any investment, there is a chance that the person you are investing in doesn't have the same endurance you do, and perhaps isn't trained to see too far in the future. One of the reasons some business owners shy away from scaling into a brand is because they do not foresee their ability to make such investments in people. This is where money and vision come in to the picture, and require a great deal of confidence in yourself. Sharing where you can go with people and getting them to buy in to your vision is an essential leader trait here. You permit money to become the balance of the external motivation needed when everything else fails.

Money Isn't a Goal. It's Leverage

Money in this stage isn't about marketing or expansion, but rather leverage. To be a successful business at this point, you've already figured out how to make money. Leverage comes from your capability to hire better talent and expand your skills. The more money you have, the less you worry about hiring someone at the cheapest rate. Instead, you look for someone who can contribute to your growth, based on their expertise and talents. You can attract more experienced and capable talent expanding your abilities and reach new clients.

The leverage can also be used to help you launch new projects in more areas or in new industries. The excess capital prompts your need to identify new verticals in order to expand. You use the capital from a growth standpoint. This is driven either by the need to avoid giving the capital to taxes or how and when to make the right move, because even the greatest of businesses can have limited expiration dates. Most business owners who pay themselves $300,000 or more in salary won't have any use for an extra $20,000 for the year. Instead, invest in the next level, making changes that will open the doors to one million dollars or five million dollars in revenue tweaks. Expanding your perspective in this way guides you to reinvest in your infrastructure, in order to be able to sustain the efforts.

The investment should be broken down first into your human capital, followed by your technology, then supported by process management and spending money to lower costs of production, such as manufacturing in-house. The expansion can only occur as the vision becomes clearer and bigger and the money continues to facilitate that gap between your vision and your existing process.

Realignment of Vision

Since there was a vision to begin with, there was a sense of direction. But now comes the time to establish direction, but not gauge it. Vision in Stage 3 is about clarity and making sure all the choices you have made to date are aligned with your chosen destination. Think of this stage as knowing you have enough fuel for the road trip ahead. You must know how far you are going and what you will need to have a successful journey to the top. The point of realigning your vision at this stage is to make sure you do not rush to move forward without the clarity of the destination. Very often, business owners want to become brands and grow to exponential numbers, yet never look far enough ahead. Instead, they just look a little bit farther, hoping to take the next phase in small increments. As a result, they forecast poorly and stay stuck in the transition. The business owner looks at everything—from taking on capital to expand, hiring more people, investing their own cash, all of which are relevant concepts at this stage—but without taking into account every aspect. They find themselves still stuck in the business at a time when it is vital for them to work on the business. The early stages of becoming a well-known brand means being able to support a transition from the business being the extension of you, into its own entity.

Be adaptive in your vision, not overly flexible. The world is ever-changing and, while the necessary steps may change along the path of executing your plan, the vision should never change. You must adapt your vision to the changing environment that is coming up. You should be alert of what is happening in your industry to ensure you stay ahead of it at all times. You should look even farther, preparing to take advantage of emerging markets based on consumer behavior and technology changes. It would be foolish to think that, in the ten to thirty years it will take you to establish your brand and empire, the world we live in won't change and that the way people get their information or reach your business will be the exact same. I have always wanted to bridge the gap between formal and self-education and start a magazine, but eventually realized that being in the online market made more sense as magazines, in general, were on the decline. Also, I saw the opportunity in the online realm of eventually leading to an app-based platform, and so on. The decisions we make, based on the future, help shape our own path instead of being a by-product of whatever the market is doing. In other words, we create the direction rather than letting external influences drive our internal changes.

Becoming a powerful brand requires a proactive attitude towards everything, rather than a reactive one. No different than the mind and its acceptance or mastery of circumstance, your business must learn to adapt to stay ahead, but you shouldn't be too flexible in what you want, as flexibility is often a weakness that stems from a lack of capacity. A core trait of successful visionaries who meritoriously build effective and multigenerational empires comes from their ability to settle for nothing less than what they want. People, like Steve Jobs, were not engineers and didn't care about limitations of engineering knew what they wanted to see happen. The same can be said for others like Elon Musk, who didn't concern himself with how profitable electrical car models should be, but instead focused on how electric cars will help reshape the consumer's desires to drive them.

An empire is no longer an extension of its CEO, but becomes a person of its own and must go through its own three-circle shifts to bring a vision to life. A CEO must integrate himself or herself into the business, to create a self-sustaining entity that no longer requires him or her to be the leader of it. It's so hard for many people to do this because, as discussed in the

Third Circle Theory, we look at the world from a third perspective—one that doesn't place you as the center of everything. Once you remove yourself from the equation, the empire becomes self-sustaining and continues to uphold its legacy.

Some of today's greatest visionaries knew what they wanted their products to do and look like and what mattered the most. Even though people on their team may have argued the possibilities of such vision, these leaders would not allow themselves to be limited by the inability of those around them or their environment, but rather only by their own lack of capacity.

Flexible = External influence choosing direction

Adaptive= Self-realization of what is necessary.

Never be flexible. Always be adaptive if you are going to see something extraordinary come to life, as the essence of "extraordinary" isn't defined by ordinary action that all people see as possible, but rather as the one action that no one believed possible.

Stage 4

The final stage that connects visionary to empire, and establishes the legacy. Personal Vision is the essence of everything started, as well as the bond between businesses and visionaries that prevents the final growth of the empire and its transition from building a brand into an empire.

The idea of legacy is a personal thought as much as it is an extension of a vision. The vision, if accepted, is in the best interest of the brand, and not in the interest of its owner. This is the stage that pushes many owners to sell their business to a larger corporation or entity that will integrate their products and services. As a result, the brand becomes part of their empire where someone else's vision has built from more confidence and a broader view of the possibilities (we discussed earlier how you yourself could buy other businesses to expand; this is the same idea, in the reverse role). That is because someone's vision is greater than the existing brand's vision, and their structures and capacity are more advanced. If the visionaries can separate their view of their legacy from the brand, then the possibilities will expand far beyond the grasp of the owner. The empire and its foundation will have been established—with the owner as its employee—but without that separation and with the need to continue the established vision and the sole driver of the momentum. The owner will selfishly prevent this transition. The word "legacy" comes in play as the time to choose if your legacy is more important than your business will be the determining factor of what happens next. A simple example is understanding that, while Walt Disney's name will forever live on through his amusement parks, characters, and movies, Mickey Mouse and many of the other characters that Disney stands for have their very own legacy and, to kids, will always just be Mickey Mouse or any other Disney character.

If you want to make an impact, you must understand what is required. This is no different than leaving behind a legacy. While most consider their children as their true legacy, those visionaries understand that the world is way too big to revolve around family and that the only way a legacy is carried on for more than one generation is because of its continuous impact through time, long past our departure from this world. Like raising a child, providing for a family, or fostering talent in people, the biggest impacts are not made by the smallest and easiest contributions, but rather by the ability to continuously improve a process until its perfection can be felt for decades and whose infrastructure can be improved upon with ease. It is the impact we make in others that is recognized, remembered, and shared, giving us the opportunity to experience true fulfillment and graduate past the Third Circle.

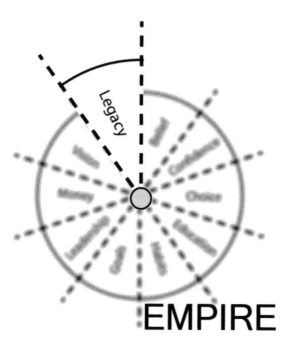

The Overnight Success Story to the Finish Line

Building a business is a sprint to the finish line, but building an empire is like a marathon. You are running in both races but building an empire requires you to think of the possibilities ahead, as the distance is significantly longer and the finish line is never in sight.

When you own a business it's easy to get excited; it's easy to look at what others are doing and say, "I can do that, too." While the hardest part may have been to get started, it is now the easiest part of your day, as you no longer have to worry about what to do but rather how well you do it. Once you have a process in place, it becomes the work ethic that drives you forward. My experience is that the majority of owners and CEO's in the earlier stages of their businesses don't seem to understand how much endurance plays a role with being successful. Instead, they focus on the idea of running as fast and as far as they can. The problem with such a mindset is that the faster runners often get tired and slow down, especially when all their energy goes into something that doesn't materialize into revenue as expected. How many times have you heard people looking at someone else's advertisements on social media and say, "That makes no sense", or "I can do better"? In reality, the question should be, "Can I sustain the intensity longer?" Many of us believe we can do better than the concepts we witness, but the true question is if can we be creative, effective, and precise to sustain this level of discipline for the years to come, not just one year. Can we sustain this even when no results come out of it for months? Can we keep running rather than slow down to take breaks? Do we have the right team, partners, and people in place to carry the baton when we become tired so that the velocity of the business isn't slowed by our limitations? These are the questions one must asked himself/herself.

Those who cannot graduate past the "business" pillar typically grow in spurts; while those who stay in this for the long haul understand it is their only way to break into the brand pillar, and eventually in the empire pillar. They aren't just relying on their ability to be energetic and intense, but they are maintaining the same momentum in the next ten years or more, despite the environment's reactions to their own actions, successes, or failures from their experience. Staying the course with intensity and not allowing the distractions to interfere helps people build brands that bloom into a long-lasting empire and create a legacy they never imagined possible.

The RADIUS model was created to help you reach farther in your grasp of the possibilities of transitioning from an idea to a product, to build a business that is validated as a brand by its customers, and finally to a stage where each brand you created can come together, forming an empire. The idea is simply to understand the connection between each pillar and the concepts located within them. Your legacy is, in the end, the by-product of the impact your empire has on those who interact with it.

Final Words

I hope you enjoyed getting an inside look into my world, my perspective, and my views on how some of today's top visionaries connect the dots forward to form some of the most currently established brands and empires. I tried to show you from my very own adaptation of *Third Circle Theory* how some of my very own companies are inter-connected, so that you can relate my life experiences to the concepts shared in *RADIUS*.

Regardless that you observe and understand my business decisions and the direction I choose to take, or that you observe one of the three hundred entrepreneurs that are teaching in the Secret Entourage Academy, there is a single element that remains consistent and true across the board, regardless of the industry or business someone is involved in. It is the core of why many of us succeed and how we do so. It is our ability to identify who we are and surround ourselves with people who amplify our purpose in this world.

Throughout my corporate career, business ownership, and entrepreneurial ventures, I have recognized a correlation not in what I did, but *how* I did it. Although people give me several titles—CEO, entrepreneur, mentor, leader, millionaire—the reality is that I am none of those things. Each of them were valid at a different part of my life, but none were the reason I transitioned from one to the next. All are titles I held at different times and in different capacities, but there was one title I held from the very beginning and continue to hold: teacher. To me being a teacher is the definition of my life purpose and as a result of its acceptance, I have been able to foster this very important talent within myself and allow those who surround me, to help create vehicles to deliver it to others. I am an educator, and have always been. I was a teacher in my leadership style when in Corporate America. I was a teacher when I educated many individuals in the luxury lifestyle world of my concierge service. And I was a teacher when I took on the role of helping to fix the access to education by introducing some of my online teachings.

I accepted that I am a teacher. As a result, I have leveraged that teaching skill to foster talent in others and allow them to become that bridge between my talent and the world through their very own talents and capacity. My greatest students are my employees and customers, and my greatest asset is their ability to choose which direction they wish to take in life—yet they choose to stand by my side. Understanding your very own purpose, talent, and capacity as shared in the pages of this book will help you become the person you need to become, so you can hold the various titles of capacity you wish for like leader, CEO, millionaire, entrepreneur, etc. Nevertheless, just remember that titles are not given, but earned. They are earned by the impact we once again make on those around us. There is a famous saying, "being at the top of the mountain is very lonely", but the top of the mountain only feels lonely for those who never realized that the journey to the top isn't a sprint, but rather a relay marathon. A marathon filled with incredible people ready to carry on the baton, which means accepting that someone else's potential and ability can exceed your own, and it should never be limited by your own aspirations. Always push people to the very limits of their capacity. Furthermore, allow them to have many breakthroughs and victories, as winning in entrepreneurship is, and always will be, a team sport.

"VISIONARIES ARE, AFTER ALL, NOTHING MORE THAN THE ARCHITECTS OF THE FUTURE, WHILE ENTREPRENEURS ARE ITS ENGINEERS. IT IS ONLY WHEN ONE EMBRACES THE OTHER THAT THE VISION, LEGACY, AND FUTURE BECOME ONE AND THE SAME, AND THE ABILITY TO CREATE YOUR VERY OWN 'RADIUS' COMES TO LIFE." – *Pejman Ghadimi*

Acknowledgements

From the bottom of my heart, I thank all of the fans and students for your continued support of the *Third Circle Theory*, *RADIUS*, and Secret Entourage. Thank you for trusting in my ability to teach you, guide you, and lead you to a better version of yourself. If it weren't for all of you, I would have never been able to live out my very own life purpose today, continuing to push the boundaries of what and how I teach.

Thanks to Alan, Navid, Andrew, Yris and all the other incredible, behind-the-scenes individuals who help support Secret Entourage and its mission worldwide. It is because of your ability to see past yourselves that we are going to be able to make a true impact in the world. Our core team continues to grow and it is in its expansion that our bond is tested the most. I am excited for the next ten years ahead and look forward to being part of your growth.

Thanks to my uncle, Parviz Monsefan, to whom I dedicated this book. I never expressed how grateful I was to be able to have a such a great father figure when I was growing up, and how incredibly generous you were in helping my mother and me have a real chance to succeed. People like you exemplify what a role model really should be like.

Thanks to Fabio Viviani for accepting to write the foreword to *RADIUS*. It was shortly after our first meeting that I immediately realized what an incredible human being you are. I don't think in my 35 years of life that I have ever met anyone who shares so much of my values going forward. I am excited for the years to come and for the evolution of our friendship.

Thank you to all the academy teachers who share my values of helping change how and what people learn. It is your commitment to excellence in your field and your willingness to educate that makes you the most incredible teachers any academy could ever ask for. We continue to grow and help more people, thanks to your generosity with your time.

Thank you to my mother, Shahla, who continues to remain a beacon of hope and inspiration. Your story and your continued devotion to being the incredible mother you are is unparalleled. The sacrifices you continue to make, and the moral and emotional support you give to everyone around you is the reason my purpose in life became teaching, so that your legacy could live on and the evolution of your words heard. I am after all nothing more than the extension of your teachings, and the observations of how you lived.

Last but not least thank you to all the incredible people out there who trust in my words and guidance to help move them forward one step closer to their goals. It is important to recognize that each of you has a choice as to whose voice you listen to and give an opportunity to, and that it is why I thank you for allowing me the opportunity to speak. A teacher can only strive if he has students, and I thank you for choosing me as your teacher.